Fast-track to Failure

a user's guide to abject misery

GARETH HARVEY

Angus&Robertson
An imprint of HarperCollins*Publishers*

AN ANGUS & ROBERTSON BOOK
An imprint of HarperCollinsPublishers

First published in Australia in 1993 by
CollinsAngus&Robertson Publishers Pty Limited (ACN 009 913 517)
A division of HarperCollinsPublishers (Australia) Pty Limited
25-31 Ryde Road, Pymble NSW 2073, Australia

HarperCollinsPublishers (New Zealand) Limited
31 View Road, Glenfield, Auckland 10, New Zealand

HarperCollinsPublishers Limited
77-85 Fulham Palace Road, London W6 8JB, United Kingdom

Distributed in the United States of America by
HarperCollins Publishers
10 East 53rd Street, New York NY 10022, USA

National Library of Australia
Cataloguing-in-Publication data:

Harvey, Gareth.
    Fast-track to failure: a user's guide to abject misery.
    ISBN 0 207 17830 5.
    1. Failure (Psychology) — Humour. 2. Australian wit and humour.
    I. Title.
A828.302

Printed in Australia by Griffin Paperbacks, Adelaide

 5 4 3 2 1
97 96 95 94 93

To my fellow non-achievers.

Contents

Preface

I AM OUTRAGED!

I am really, really angry!

I have just read this book, this so-called *Fast-track to Failure* and I want to sue somebody!

You see, I am the un-named failure whose life has been lifted as the case study for this pitiful example of the publisher's art.

I have been plagiarised! I have been dissected! Dissembled!

But what do my bleats from the abyss matter to those responsible for this perfidy? What does the world care about Amis E. Rableman? Is it of interest to anyone that I am living proof of the power of negative thinking?

No! I know that when you have selfishly achieved your own failure, when you have secured your doom, you will think little of Amis E. Rableman — even though it is this unauthorised autobiography which will have given you the tools to sink so spectacularly in the sea of life!

And, worse than all of this, you will know nothing of my poetry about chickens.

Yes, the unkindest cut of all is that this very publisher has chosen to print the following swill over my major work — *Heidegger and the Hen*! It is sad, but somehow to be expected by artists like myself, that you will never become familiar with Amis E. Rableman — the Poet Laureate of Poultry.

No, you are about cheap thrills, swift sensations — you care only about becoming the worst quickest, with no thought about who you are displacing in your downward scramble.

Well — regardless of the priceless gems which this author has so shabbily stolen from my treasury of torpidity — you will soon find that failure is not that simple.

Failure doesn't just happen!

True failure is an intricate coupling of genetic deficiency and hard work — there are no short cuts to becoming your own worst case scenario!

But don't listen to me. No-one ever does. Everyone copies me — from Dan Quayle to Eeyore — but no-one, before this book, has attempted such a full-blooded photocopy of my persona!

Perhaps I won't sue after all. Perhaps the only threat I will leave with you, the reader who conspires to be worse than me, is the promise that if you buy this book then somewhere, in a public place, in front of your friends, I will walk up and pretend to be your father!

Hah, hah, hah! The Curse of Amis E. Rableman!

Now back to my life's work:

> *Your coxcomb blows in the breeze,*
> *The henhouse fumes make me sneeze,*
> *I fondle an egg, as I think of Heidegg . . .*

Amis E. Rableman, 1993

The Power of Negative Thinking

Introduction

Failure is the most common of human conditions. We all fail, but some of us more disastrously than others. Why is that? Why have some people 'got' something that others haven't in the field of human non-achievement? In short — is there a way of fast-tracking to failure?

The answer is YES!, and you're holding it. The power of negative thinking is in your hands! Approaching Life's major problems with an attitude guaranteed to provide the wrong solutions can be achieved if you follow this step-by-step field guide to failure.

Think of this book as a hitchhiker's guide to a demolition derby.

Obviously there are specialist failures out there who concentrate on specific life areas in which to underachieve — mountain climbing, abseiling, deep sea diving — but usually they don't last long. This book is designed with the common or garden variety of failure in mind. Its purpose is simply to help you become a walking disaster area in Life's major categories: at work; at home; in love and marriage; in public places; even in death.

Specific failure skills are outlined in each life area to assist you on your downward plunge. You will, for example, learn techniques like:

☞ How to recognise success and avoid it;
☞ How to become a social cripple;
☞ How to embarrass yourself at work;

and, most importantly,

☞ How to spot a fool a mile off. And imitate him!

Quizzes are provided to help you pinpoint areas where you naturally shine as a failure and those in which you need further work.

All failures, especially novitiates, need negative reinforcement. Accordingly, you will find case studies of outstanding failure types to be used as role models. You will observe directly how others have taken an active role in their own decline, how they have turned Life's little pitfalls into yawning chasms. You will learn from these case studies what constitutes success and what constitutes failure, and how to unerringly choose the latter. You will learn how to lose what others have lost and feel really bad about it.

> **T**here *IS* a methodology to misery and you *CAN* learn to make the wrong choices at all the way-stations from birth to death.

But perhaps the major lesson you will learn from these pages is the insidious nature of opportunity. As you work your way through these chapters, you will gain a sixth sense about opportunity, and you will learn the art of being out when it knocks. If it does nothing else, this book will act as your insurance policy against opportunity ever happening to you.

Obviously even the most profound Fast-track Failure risks relapsing into success and self-fulfilment, so there is a special concluding section containing a set of exercises designed to help you cope with joy, so that — in times of such crisis — you can look inward, into the deepest recesses of your soul, and find . . . nothing.

Yes, reading this book will be a unique voyage into your dark side. You will discover things about yourself that will drive you to the observation deck of a large skyscraper. Then you will discover a few more things about yourself.

Then you will jump.

Part I

FAILURE IN THE WORKFORCE

Becoming Unemployable

Chapter 1

It is what takes up most of our day. The job! Society is a great seething mass of jobs, of opportunity, of success stories! Your place in the civilised world — the sort of men or women you meet and those you have passionate sex with; the type of car you drive and the number of cylinders beneath its deep red exterior and the 'Porsche' symbol; the size of your house, and the size of your servant's house — will be determined by your job.

It's a pity about that really . . .

The job market is also the perfect place to begin your descent into the hell of lost opportunity.

Picking the Worst Job

You must begin by giving serious thought to the worst job for you. Don't worry, there are plenty out there! Try becoming the talking clock (for practice, when asked for the time by strangers, say 'At the third stroke it will be . . .'), working in an advertising agency, being a loans manager at a bank, doing PR for a tobacco company, or acting in TV commercials for haemorrhoid creams (as a test, try saying to a mirror 'Darling, good news! The doctor says he doesn't have to operate!').

There is no shortage of jobs that pretty well guarantee a lifetime of misery and take the struggle out of becoming a failure in the workplace. But perhaps you are looking for a special job. One which will have you dreaming of the next life.

That one profession with your name on it which, when raised, causes guests to change the subject at dinner parties and embarrasses your children.

If you are gripped by a sense of your own potential insignificance and want to hear the phrase 'I thought they had machines to do that!' often — so be it!

But first you must stumble through the job interview.

Perturbing Personal Deportment

The ability to create a fetid first impression on a potential employer through the simple technique of Perturbing Personal Deportment (PPD) is a skill which comes naturally to many people.

There are those who, when they speak, make it sound as if they are choking. To try this during your job interview, let the tension you are feeling as you stare into your potential employer's eyes grip your windpipe. Then speak:

'Maihh — (gasp) — nem ess Her . . . rrry Smth!'
(My name is Henry Smith.)

Or there are those who have learnt how to talk and dribble at the same time:

'Pbbbllzze gbbblibb mbbmme blllis jblob!'
(Please give me this job!)

Treating the spoken word as something which has to be dredged from some nether region of the throat through a combination of hacking and nasal wheezing is a particularly fine talent practised by some:

'Haarrrggghh paaaasccchhhht ashitoooyoooo saicchggh?'
(Half-past two you say?)

Of course, nothing beats scratching violently; twitching; nail biting (which with only a little training can come to resemble thumb-sucking); and public ear-cleaning (preferably with an implement chosen at random from your potential employer's desk — a paper clip, pen or scissors).

Also, your eye-line is important during the job interview. Make sure it never hits the horizontal. Staring a little above or below your potential employer's eyes can create the distinct impression that you have spotted something nasty on his forehead, or an errant nostril hair.

But PPD is not enough in and of itself to guarantee failure in the job interview . . . for that you have to exhibit not merely cosmetic, but structural personality defects. Aside from questions of personal hygiene, could you actually do the job required of you?

Here is a quick quiz to determine which category of ineptitude you fall into.

Do You Have What

1. When asked directions by little old ladies in the street do you:

    (a) Respond directly and intelligently, with just a touch of compassion because you have a mother too?

    (b) Hand over all your money and scream 'For God's sake please don't kill me!'?

    (c) Smile a superior smile because you *do* know the way, but you're damned if you're going to share that kind of information?

    (d) Burst into tears?

2. When you bump into a chair at home do you:

    (a) Shake yourself, silently chide yourself for your clumsiness, and chuckle because if this is the worst that happens to you today who are you to complain?

    (b) Apologise to the chair?

    (c) Drop-kick it?

    (d) Cry?

3. When you see a snail crossing your path, do you:

    (a) Wonder at its patience and see in its steady progress a modus operandi for your life?

    (b) Look at it and see yourself reincarnated?

    (c) Crush it with your shoe?

    (d) Weep?

It Doesn't Take?

4. When asked by a personnel manager interviewing you for a job 'why are you here?', do you:

    (a) State clearly your ambition, emphasising that it is tempered by a desire to 'put something back into the community'?

    (b) Whimper 'because I always wanted to meet someone as important as a personnel manager'?

    (c) Say 'The opportunity to tread on the little guy'?

    (d) Bleat weakly in the corner?

5. On spotting a framed photograph of your potential employer's wife, do you:

    (a) Compliment him on his wife's dress sense and the high quality of the framing?

    (b) Ask him if she is his mother?

    (c) Ask him, while stroking the photograph suggestively, whether she is his daughter?

    (d) Sigh hopelessly 'I wish someone would marry me'?

If you answered mostly (a) in the quiz you are probably lying to yourself. Type A job applicants are well-rounded, well-adjusted, well . . . just about everything you're not.

No, it is more likely you meant to answer (b) but are in fact functionally illiterate (a common trait among Type B job applicants).

TYPE B: HIRE ME —
I'LL MAKE YOU LOOK GOOD!

If you answered mostly (b) in the above quiz, chances are that you are a Hire-Me-I'll-Make-You-Look-Good type; the sort of person so bad at your job that all those around you shine by comparison.

Every office *needs* a Type B failure, a yardstick by which every other employee's ineptitude can be measured.

Type B workers are essential to the modern corporate structure because there always has to be someone to take the blame, someone to be the worst!

From the strength of the office coffee to an abysmal profit sheet, you will invariably find a Type B failure at the bottom of the problem. Someone to point the finger at, someone to shout at gratuitously.

If, during your interview, you present to an employer as having the potential to be the office whipping boy (or girl), you stand a good chance of not only getting through the job interview but being poached by one of the many firms of heel-hunters currently seeking out the hapless and the inept on behalf of middle-ranking executives. Don't worry too much; it is all part of the incompetent feeling comfortable with their own incompetence! You will still get your chance to prove your remarkable ineptitude in the great professional sand pit of life.

But perhaps you answered (c) in the quiz.

TYPE C: THE OFFICE KICK BOXER

If you are an Office Kick Boxer you probably answered (c) in the above quiz (presuming of course you did not dispense with the formality of learning to read on your irresistible surge to the top). Your type constitutes the major category of corporate failure, so isolating yourself amongst the mob will not be easy.

But do not get depressed — remember, **YOU HAVE THIS BOOK!**

Using the following helpful hints (get someone smaller than you to read them aloud as you drop-kick them around the room), you can modify your own mediocrity to assure yourself of truly outstanding under-achievement, and secure your placement in a bottom-rung job.

The truly spectacular Office Kick Boxer is a disciple of himself, a self-appointed prophet of profit, a person who has read one too many 'How to Succeed' books.

Your opening sally is to look your potential employer in the eyes, giving the latter a moment to consider your daunting personality, before violently shaking the proffered hand and growling:

'Greed is best.'

Prior to this of course, you have spent quality time snickering at the other poor souls who have turned up for *your* job interview. Deep in your heart you know the only reason they are occupying valuable office space is to satisfy Equal Opportunity Regulations.

You have been listening to motivational tapes on your walkman but have murmured between tape changes: 'I don't know why some of you even bother!'

You asked your neighbour with apparent politeness: 'Do you realise what this job involves?'

And finally, on first meeting your potential employer, you inform him that if he really wants to go ahead with the charade of interviewing others, you've already spoken to them in the waiting room on his behalf and narrowed the field down to two.

As early as possible into the job interview, state the level at which you see yourself stepping on to the corporate ladder, the sort of work you would prefer *not* to do, and your favourite make of car.

The utter confidence you feel at this moment is breathtaking. **THIS COMPANY NEEDS YOU! BADLY!** So much so that you decide to start now; by coaching the potential employer on how to conduct a really good job interview.

Should you meet a current employee of the company (who may have popped into the boss's office for a signature) you immediately impose your superiority on this obvious example of human insignificance. You ignore the other's extended hand, apart from placing a business card in it, and quietly explain that there is no need to affect cordiality, adding:

'I'm sure we'll be at each other's throats soon enough, we don't want this hanging over us do we!'

When the soon-to-be-swamped employee clumsily attempts to discover the secrets of your success, asking: 'What school did you go to?'

You reply: 'Wouldn't you like to know!'

'The school of hard knocks', you add menacingly as soon as you see his back.

Your bravura is brimming over; you have seen your first enemy and stared him down.

You return to the job interview at hand, sprinkling your answers liberally with phrases from *Success in 6 Working Days* like:

'Hire me and you'll be investing in your future'
and:

'I'm a can-do individual!'

You also seize control of the interview.

You spot in a transparently inane question from your potential employer a chance to exhibit your ability to instantly dominate any situation. In answer to the query you simply nod in an authoritatively dismissive way and say: 'Next question.'

The more practised Kick Boxing individual works the interview more and more, wielding well-memorised tactics like the use of the potential employer's first name, or an abbreviation of it:

'Sure Chuck, good question . . .'
or:

'Can I call you Lizzie . . .',

and picking up the framed photograph of the potential employer's spouse while commenting conspiratorially:

'Isn't sex just the ultimate power trip?'
or:

'She looks like she's got a great body!'

Finally the ceremonial interview draws to a close with the totally over-awed potential employer asking:

'Why are you seeking this job?'

It is a wan question, but in the convivial climate you have so methodically created, you decide to answer:

'Look I could say "the pursuit of raw power"'
(laugh a little),

'"The chance to play office politics", "the opportunity to tread on the little guy". But no — I honestly believe this company *needs* me, otherwise I wouldn't be here.'

On leaving the potential employer to wonder at your intellectual supremacy, tell his secretary to confirm your next job interview, and while she is doing so, assure her that her job is safe if you join the company — asking her if she likes working for younger men. Her task successfully completed, promise her a raise and ask what she earns now. Then laugh . . .

On the way out of the building wait until the elevator is full before asking your neighbour whether the company has an office kick boxing team.

Though the above type characterises the preponderance of corporate losers, the common or garden variety vocational malcontent if you like, there also exists with this approach the potential to become a flop of monumental, possibly historical proportions. Look at business tycoons of the 1980s for inspiration.

But perhaps you answered (d) in the quiz.

TYPE D: HIRE ME OR I'LL KILL MYSELF

If you answered mostly (d) in the quiz you are the job applicant type known by its technical title of Hire Me Or I'll Kill Myself.

To potential employers, the only logical explanation for the presence of you (as a Hire-Me-Or-I'll-Kill-Myself individual) in their office is that you turn up to job interviews as a way of meeting people, or you believe you have turned up for some kind of therapy for a problem which is beyond the experience or imagination of the potential employer.

Anything, thinks your potential employer, except an expectation that you might actually be considered for the advertised position!

Which is truly unfortunate, because you in fact turn up for job interviews armed not simply with the desire to work but with the psychological equivalent of a large calibre hand-gun which you mean to use on yourself if you fail.

The job is everything! The way out! The ticket to ride!

Apart from answering (d) above, measure yourself against the following profile to double-check your 'job or death' mentality.

Type D Profile

1 As a prospective employee you are so terrified of saying the wrong thing during the job interview that you remain silent and thus give the outward impression that you believe the potential employer is talking to someone else. This becomes a vicious circle — as staring blankly at the potential employer while still trying to think of the right thing to say reinforces the initial impression created above.

Finally, so gripped by the overwhelming desire to say *anything* to stop the potential employer looking past you (convinced now that there *must* be someone else in the room), you attempt to speak, only to find that your tongue has dried to the roof of your mouth and all you can utter are grunts.

2 You slavishly fondle the potential employer's desk ornaments while the latter is asking questions. Apart from stroking office bric-a-brac, you will often feverishly brush the chair on which you are sitting to remove lint, and scuff the office carpet with your shoes to rid it of what appears to be a patch of dried glue.

3 Finally you try appealing to the potential employer's human side: you employ tactics such as throwing yourself upon the potential employer and weeping 'I'm depending on this job!'

Ordinarily, while having very little visible effect on the potential employer, such behaviour will cause *you* to undergo a near-religious experience, as evidenced by a soft moaning, a clasping of hands and rocking backwards and forwards on your chair. Ensure that you genuflect in front of the potential employer's desk before backing out of the office.

Unfortunately the last approach (appealing to the employer's human side) is an almost certain guarantee that the job opportunity will be withdrawn from the employment market before being offered to you. You see, the secret of it all is this:

Humans have no human side.

Death, it appears, is your only option.

But perhaps you refused the earlier quiz altogether because such imperialist notions of crass competition are beyond your enlightened thinking and are simply antiquated vestiges of an exploitative age.

The Oh Wow! Individual

Perhaps the most foolproof approach you can take to becoming unemployable is by indicating to all potential employers that you want to save the world, that you care about the future of humanity. That you care, period. It is, as mentioned, a simple approach to failure in the job-market and one best combined with another strategy (eg in following chapter see 'Zealotry as a Means to Zero Popularity'). But sometimes simple is best, and this technique may have your name on it.

Rather than shake the hand of the potential employer as she enters the office, hug and kiss her in the European fashion. Move swiftly to extol the potential employer's surface virtues:

'You have kind eyes.'

The Oh Wow! individual senses a strong psychic connection between him and the potential employer, saying (though it could simply be thought):

'I know you!'

You immediately indicate your confidence in human nature and the inherent goodness of humankind. Gripping the framed photograph on the potential employer's desk, you shed a sympathetic tear and exclaim:

'I'*m* in a charity plan for third-world families too!'

When the potential employer explains how important her company is to the well-being of the planet, you *believe* her, and listen with rapt attention — occasionally whispering phrases like:

'Oh wow!'

and:

'That's so wonderful!'

You tend to stare deep into a potential employer's eyes for minutes at a time without blinking. Other traits include nodding feverishly and earnestly as the potential job is outlined. Then you ask the potential employer to outline the company's environmental position, making it obvious that you consider the company has an environmental position.

Finally you are asked to speak about yourself, your reasons for seeking the job and why you should be hired. You reply:

'Office harmony — the spirituality of the workplace!'

activating your metaphysical link with the potential employer to use the ensuing silence positively.

You continue joyfully, explaining that you spent summer learning to test the workplace for the presence of radon gas and asbestos, and how to check ozone levels. You know a wonderfully pure brand of mineral water for the office water cooler and you believe productivity is really less important than peace of mind — you suggest that perhaps the sound of rushing streams could be piped throughout the building to enhance the collective oneness. Your optimism and conviction are obviously getting through, as your and the potential employer's moments of silence together become more and more profound:

'Desks are so regimented, why do you think we have wars?'

you proceed enthusiastically:

'Have you ever thought of futons?'

and:

'I strongly recommend that you form the staff into life-experience groups, like office families.'

and:

'Hierarchy is such a fascist concept, I can see in your eyes you agree with me. Why not call all employees just "brother" or "sister" so that titles don't interfere with their job satisfaction?'

Finally, suggest that your salary, together with all the staff wages, be put into a single bank account to which everyone has access:

'Don't you see? We would just use what we needed, and what was left could be sent to support poor families in India!'

You leave the potential employer's office ecstatic, hugging her firmly and spontaneously offering your Atlantis crystal and current Shirley MacLaine book, saying:

'Read it, everything will become clear!'

The Oh Wow! technique is simple but unparalleled in its effectiveness.

You see potential employers often consider employing members of most other classifications of professional incompetence, but they just *will not* employ loons.

Aside from the methods discussed so far, there are some miscellaneous formulas for free-form failure: gems which will jaundice your job prospects.

☞ Imply you are a committed activist of some sort. Wear a T-shirt to the interview, emblazoned with:

'People before profits' or 'Die yuppie scum!'

☞ Explain that you don't really want the job — you are doing a psychology degree. Then ask the potential employer whether he enjoys dominating people.

☞ Ask whether the company has a policy about employing ex-prisoners. When the potential employer asks why, stare at her fixedly and growl:

'Don't push me!'

A useful adjunct to the last strategy is refusing to answer various of the potential employer's questions about your previous jobs on the grounds that you might incriminate yourself.

☞ Ask the potential employer if there is a bar in her office while gripping the front of her desk tightly.

☞ Ask the potential employer if he has read *Portnoy's Complaint*.

Whatever mode of misery you have chosen, whichever fast-track to failure in the job interview you have utilised, you can gauge your performance by measuring it against the following scene.

Your potential employer is either convulsing in fury, or is seized by paroxysms of laughter as you leave — all semblance of control is gone. As you walk towards the elevators, the ringing of hysterical mirth accompanies you. It seems the potential employer decided early in the job interview to let the rest of the staff in on the joke and had the proceedings broadcast through the PA.

But this is not enough. To truly enter the stratosphere of professional catastrophe, the would-be failure must take this ignominious start and turn it into something.

Something worse . . .

How to Fail Spectacularly at Work

Chapter 2

*T*he workplace is the scene of most failure in the Western world. But in the bedlam of collective failure, amidst the hubbub of mediocrity, where everyone is too busy failing to notice whose toes they are treading on, it is difficult to sink below the pack and become a truly remarkable failure. To achieve big-time doom one must be sophisticated; and above all, to fail utterly at work, one must be perceptive.

The spectacularly dull young person must be able to quickly dissect the anatomy of a failure — so he can repeat it. You must learn how to look at mistakes people have made in the past — so you can make them again.

> *Y*ou have to limit your horizons, fear success, shy away from responsibility. If you are knocked down, you must learn the art of staying there!

The starting point for professional failure is pessimism. Take the following case study.

Professional Pessimism

A particularly proficient Fast-track Failure has just received a letter offering him a job. It is a very common, quite ordinary letter which reads, in part:

'Following your interview with the undersigned I am pleased to offer you the position of mail boy with our company. It is a position from which many of this company's top executives rose to their current status . . .'

However, in the mind of our Failure there has to be a catch — and thus he rewrites the letter in his head on the way to his first day at work:

'Dear Loser,'

it *really* begins, he convinces himself gloomily,

'Be under no illusions that the position offered herein is a stepping stone to anything else in this company. You failed to impress the undersigned of your proficiency at even the most basic motor functions. You are an example of all that is wrong with the education system these days. You are scarcely sentient!

'However, it appears that our company could profit financially by hiring you under a recently announced Federal Government Assistance Scheme. In this vein, and in a spirit of utter greed on our part, you are offered the following position with this company. It is a position which, if you were capable of comprehending it, would generally be described as a dead-end job.'

'P.S.'

The Fast-track Failure adds his own icy postscript as he alights from the bus:

'I also felt it would be amusing to watch you try to work.'

'Yes,' thinks our professional pessimist, *'I have sullied myself even taking this job!'* Then he thinks about something someone once said about turning even a bad start into something.

'Something worse',

says our pessimist aloud to a 'Don't Walk' signal.

But right away another placating platitude pops into his brain:

'At least I have my foot in the door!'

'It will probably require amputation', he thinks unhappily as he briefly becomes a sidewalk impediment to his fellow commuters.

He buys a coffee just before he reaches work and mentions to the waitress that Thomas Edison was once a mail boy like him. The waitress examines him carefully.

Then she laughs.

But nothing is helping our pessimist. No matter how much negative reinforcement he puts himself through as he walks past the front door and towards the elevators, there is the undeniable truth to deal with.

He has a job.

Now our case study above may be one of those with a special talent for outrageous failure, but it is more likely that he will just be another grey face in the crowd, that he simply does not have the drive to achieve vocational catastrophe.

The tragedy is that he, like most of us, is closer to being utterly repulsive to his boss than he may imagine.

There are many routes to failure in the workplace, and most achieve their goals by a combination of techniques.

Nevertheless, to avoid confusion let us break the field down in order to properly examine the individual aspects of a certifiable career-loser.

Dressed for Distress

In love, in life, at work — power dressing is the name of the game. But some achieve the reverse — tailored impotence. They dress for distress. These are the kinds of people one spies from afar and feels more comfortable because people like them exist.

HE His trouser legs sit just above his ankles and his new shirt is one of those colours appropriately known as 'off white', but which could perhaps be even better described as 'unlaundered'. His socks are paisley and match his paisley clip-on tie. The effect is framed by a three-piece suit to which its makers in Hong Kong have affixed a label 'Made in Italy'. His hair is shorn in a distinctive fashion, meant to express his rugged individuality but which in reality looks as though he has yet to master the art of shaving, or has fallen victim to a job training scheme at the hairdresser.

SHE The centrepiece of her ensemble, the point at which an observer's attention is inevitably focused, is her mascara. It is so overdone that she can hardly keep her eyes open. The down side of this is that she looks chemically dependent; the up side is that she burns 300 calories every time she blinks, and has developed highly muscled eyelids which are reputed to be very attractive to Mongolian yak herders. Her perfume is so overpowering that it gives vermin in the building fair warning of her approach. Any rats remaining as she enters her place of work are seen to totter behind partitions, while cockroaches plunge themselves into the nearest coffee maker in order to end it all mercifully. Her hair is coiffed in a modern style with a setting gel endorsed by Margaret Thatcher — while her clothes are highly litigious.

Desk Ornaments and You

Some people live in the firm belief that their professional workplace has to *say* something about them; that a desk has to sit there silently commenting on its occupant.

The truth is that the first step in transforming one's workplace into a living hell and being relegated to the role of office coffee table by one's boss, is to vandalise one's professional geography so that it becomes more billboard than bench space.

As a Desk-ornament Devotee you hang gaudy items of 'sentimental' value around your desk. The garter you wore when high school broke up; the snowstorm you bought on that special holiday to Wollongong; the polaroid of your pet guinea pig.

The photograph of your partner with a photograph of Tom Jones.

As a Desk-ornament Devotee you also have a fetish for useless desk equipment, which you constantly fondle as you work:

☞ electric sticky-tape dispensers;
☞ desk calendars that keep coffee warm;
☞ a stapler that plays 'Blue Moon'.

A more sophisticated Exterior Desk-designer will complete the effect created by hanging postcards everywhere. So many in fact that work colleagues come to the inescapable conclusion that the occupant has written postcards to herself and pinned them up in a pitiful attempt to prove she does have friends!

Zealotry and Zero Popularity

Something about the modern workplace seems to attract this distinctive form of professional failure. Perhaps jobs are too hard these days. Perhaps work is so mentally taxing that it affects the brain in hitherto unknown ways. In any event there is no denying the rapid increase in the number of Workplace Zealots in recent years.

In order to become a Workplace Zealot you should join a bizarre religious cult — though you may, if you wish, come up with a brand new belief system completely on your own.

The most important thing, however, is to bring your dogma to work — and preach it to the unconverted!

Your faith in your illogical theology is so monotonous and your parroting of your personal prophet is so predictable that the moment an associate says 'Hello' she knows she will hear (yet again!) how the world was created exactly five thousand, two hundred and twenty-three years, one hundred and sixteen days, four hours and thirty-five minutes ago.

Capture your co-workers in the elevator and instead of idle banter, ask who will be saved in October, when the Earth spontaneously immolates.

Other colleagues can ask the simplest question of you, the Apprentice Religious Loon, only to have their deepest suspicions about you confirmed. For example:

> **Innocent Co-worker: 'Where is the water cooler?'**
>
> **Workplace Zealot: 'The water cooler is where you would like it to be, for a water cooler is not made of metal and fluid, but of desire and need.'**
>
> **Innocent Co-worker: 'Which way to the bathroom?'**
>
> **Workplace Zealot: 'The bathroom has many realities.'**
>
> **Innocent Co-worker: 'Can I borrow your stapler?'**
>
> **Workplace Zealot: 'The notion of possession is one you must discard if you are to reach the higher plane.'**

Colleagues soon discover that you, the resident crackpot, have a meaningless metaphor for mankind's spiritual fate in every office event; an allusion to Sodom and Gomorrah in the state of repair of the electric pencil sharpener; an indication of satanic revenge in the *Financial Review* meteorological section.

And conclusive proof of God's existence in the fact that the coffee machine makes coffee!

I'm Infectious

The next classification of those marked for vocational failure are people who seem to go out of their way to convince their co-workers that they are infectious. The Infectious Person does this for sympathy and for conversation, but unfortunately does not seem to realise that nothing will isolate him more in the workplace than if his colleagues believe they stand a good chance of catching a disease from him.

The Infectious Person manages to turn casual office conversations to the topic of obscure medical conditions:

Healthy Co-worker: 'Do you think Bob's going out with Dianne?'

Infectious Person: 'I don't know, but have you heard of Diana Syndrome — it's a usually incurable form of athlete's foot.'

Healthy Co-worker: 'How about your last accounts payable report?'

Infectious Person: 'Yes . . . did you know there are also reports which indicate bubonic plague may be back?'

Healthy Co-worker: 'I wish they'd fix this water cooler!'

Infectious Person: 'So do I — if any of us catches arid-area gingivitis we're going to need as much water as we can get.'

As an Infectious Person you should spend suspiciously long periods of time in the bathroom, and continually ask work mates to cover for you while you visit the 'specialist'. Take vast quantities of pills publicly, and in casual conversation indicate that you believe a value-for-money health insurance plan is one you use regularly.

During lunchtime banter, raise topics from a medical dictionary about the treatment of rare and unpleasant diseases.

Make yourself exceptionally familiar with hospitals, and occasionally mention operations you have seen while 'waiting'.

The truly sophisticated Hypochondriac from Hell asks work mates if they know of a life insurance plan which accepts the terminally ill. Or when colleagues ask you where you are spending Christmas, just gaze at them and weep.

Repulsing the Boss

Now that you have isolated yourself among your work colleagues, you must begin a parallel action on your boss. Many of the techniques above are helpful in convincing your superior of your personal and professional paucity, but there are a few other reasons you can give your boss to make him absolutely convinced of your insignificance.

JUST SAY NO

Careers are made and lost on first impressions.

The first impression a boss has of a Just-Say-No individual is revulsion.

Then nausea.

Then complete abhorrence.

Because the first thing the Wanting Worker has said to the boss is

'No' . . .

No ifs, buts, or maybes!

He just said 'No'.

or:

'No can do sir.'

or:

'Sorry, you picked the wrong person.'

and occasionally:

'Why, when it's been done before?'

In any event, to become a Just-Say-No individual, upon being given your first task you should stare the boss in the eyes and explain firmly that it just can't be done.

But there is no challenge in simply being incompetent, anyone can be that — and many, many, already are! No — you are not going to be a vague itch in some remote region of your boss's mind.

You are going to be a fully fledged FOCUS OF LOATHING!

HOW TO BECOME THE OFFICE LICKSPITTLE

The basic definition of an Office Lickspittle is a person who is very, very bad at what they are employed to do, but very, very apologetic about it. It is what Type B job applicants (Hire-Me-I'll-Make-You-Look-Good) invariably become.

As an Office Lickspittle, you soon realise the extent of your own incompetence — Lickspittles are not blind, just dumb. When you gauge that your boss is seriously angry with you, invite him around to dinner to 'meet the wife and kids'.

Then spend the evening engaged not in carefree banter designed to help him forget workaday worries, but instead quote him to the other dinner party guests at every turn:

☞ 'Look, the Boss has a way of dealing with that! He always says "Bums belong on the streets, not on my chairs!"'

or:

☞ 'Yes, couldn't agree more . . . as the Boss says "The only people who should be taxed are those who don't deserve to have money in the first place."'

or:

☞ 'So I'm in the office, wondering what to do with this hideous report from Jones and up comes the Boss and sacks him on the spot! Hah, hah, hah, hah!'

By the end of the night the boss has almost squirmed off his chair in embarrassment, though he has in the process made one important discovery: if he ever lost both legs he could walk unassisted on his buttocks.

Reacting to the contempt in which you are being held by the boss at work, bring him gifts in an attempt to ingratiate yourself.

Find out what the boss likes by rummaging through his home garbage bin, and occasionally if you find something you are sure he didn't mean to throw out, return it to him.

Record the boss's instructions to you, explaining: 'this is so I can replay them to myself and make sure I get it right!'

Whenever you are ushered into the hallowed ground of the boss's office, genuflect. Many Office Lickspittles ask for a splinter from the boss's desk to keep as an icon in a small glass bottle.

The Office Lickspittle is also proficient at affecting 'crisis mode', as if the future of the company is dangling in the balance every time *you* have to make a decision. And so, regardless of whether it is 'one or two lumps in your coffee?' or 'the building is under nuclear attack' the Lickspittle will, in a complex series of histrionics, deal loudly and forcefully with the problem and thus bring the entire corporation back from the brink.

But perhaps one of the Office Lickspittle's greatest talents is the 'Grand Guilt Tour'.

Whenever you think you are about to join the ranks of the unemployed, bring relatives in 'to see where you work'. Use the cover of your kin to be grossly over-familiar with the boss and attempt to secure your position with the company:

'The Boss and I have really got this company moving again!'

you inform your grandmother in front of the boss.

'Yep, he's often said to me "I don't know what I'd do if you left!" That's why I felt so sure we could afford the operation for you Nanna . . .'

As well as simpering to your boss at work, attempt to engineer a social relationship with him. Join the boss's health club, not to exercise but just to be with him in the spa and sauna. Or go to the boss's favourite restaurant and try to catch his eye all evening by waving earnestly or sending him cheap liqueurs.

After work join the boss in the little bar he goes to in order to forget that people like you work for him. Once there, read the boss memos you have written that day, or tell conspiratorial stories about your colleagues. Appoint yourself as the boss's 'eyes and ears' to keep him abreast of the dark secrets of office politics, every last rumour — however blatantly untrue:

'I don't know if you know,' you say, eyes narrowing, 'but Jones may be working for the enemy.'

And finally, call the boss on weekends . . .

Just to say hello.

If you have followed the above master plan for misery, your job is now a living hell. The office wit has catalogued the most creative invective hurled at you. A collection has been taken to buy a separate water cooler for you. The Tax Department is harassing you, giving their reason as 'un-named sources'.

One morning you find a kilo of green prawns taped under your desk.

Your tasks have become more and more menial, and finally you are trusted with nothing apart from polishing telephones and manually shredding documents.

Well done!

You are well on the way to becoming a Fast-track Failure!

Part II

Failure in the Public World

How to Become a Social Cripple

Chapter 3

While ill-breeding or the odd grey piece in your genetic jigsaw puzzle can contribute to the transition from would-be social butterfly to indisputable asocial moth, becoming a fully-fledged, card-carrying Social Cripple requires serious commitment.

Helping you attain that skill is the primary aim of this chapter.

Essential to the Fast-track Failure is the knack of totally and irretrievably alienating oneself at a dinner party.

Your own dinner party is a good starting point for the slide into obscurity and contempt. It is familiar ground, and while you still have friends it is important to use them.

And it is important for them to KNOW they are being used.

So let us look at a chronology of the world's worst dinner party with a view to picking up a few clues.

The Cookin' Fool:
How to Become Social Cripple Type 1

The scene is an otherwise normal house, apart from the presence of you, the Fast-track Failure, who, in the area of ennui-causing-entertainment, is referred to by the correct title of the Cookin' Fool. You have somehow managed to entice a group of otherwise normal individuals to a dinner party. (Sure you had one 'witty' RSVP which read in part '. . . would love to, but I had already promised my cat I'd stay home and check her for fleas that night', but then there's one in every crowd isn't there?)

The guests arrive full of hope, infected with optimism. In this most basic form of social interaction — the sharing of food — something stirs in their hearts which harks back to the solidarity of their ancient forebears gathered around the campfire, united against the dangers of the night, sharing the common goal of making the world a better place.

Hah!

ENFORCED TEMPERANCE

The guests mill in the lounge room, around the oil-heater, unaware that the only danger of the night is currently being spawned in the kitchen.

Expectation is running high among the guests that they will be offered a drink, totally unaware that you are innately adept at the art of enforced temperance.

Central to this practice is the knowledge that when placed in a situation of probable and imminent boredom, most people reach for a drink to help ease the pain.

There are a variety of strategies for enforcing temperance.

Usually it can be achieved through inadequate planning:

Innocent Guest: 'Gin and tonic?'
Cookin' Fool: 'Gin? . . . damn!'

---

followed by a simpering apology that will become the hallmark of the evening.

But tonight you are going to use the 'Ghastly-and-lurid Cocktail Approach'. This technique of enforced temperance begins by turning to your guests and announcing:

'I'll mix you all a Rainbow Warrior!'

It soon transpires that a 'Rainbow Warrior' is a Cookin' Fool concoction comprising two parts creme de menthe, and one part cherry brandy, blackberry nip and advocaat.

Topped up with diet lemonade.

'Free range advocaat!'

you quip cheerfully as you hand the repulsive drinks to their desperate but nevertheless unwilling recipients, who are starting to feel like participants in a science project.

But in such an atmosphere, enforced temperance can only last so long before the will crumbles, and finally, in the form of sickly sips, your guests imbibe their first alcohol. They grip their glasses with a firmness which can only come from the prospect that, hideous though its contents may be, it may be the extent of the night's available anaesthetic.

THE ART OF MIND-NUMBING CONVERSATION

Pre-dinner conversation, if you work the room correctly, will get off to a faltering start and then peter out altogether.

A Cookin' Fool is a master of the unique art of mind-numbing conversation, a complex and entwined series of banalities which must be used in the correct manner for the full effect to be gained:

☞ 'You know, maybe it's just me but don't you think the way the bubbles go up in a water cooler tells us something about man's inhumanity to man?'

☞ 'I wonder how many drops of rain are falling on the Earth at this exact moment?'

☞ 'Do any of you sometimes just stare at a lizard and wonder?'

The real magic of mind-numbing conversation is to expect an answer to your questions.

Exhibiting a native talent you have in this area, and unconsciously seeking to create some activity in the room during one of the lengthening periods of silence, you absent-mindedly activate a metronome. The effect of this is, of course, to emphasise the gradual passing of time and highlight the gaps where discourse would ordinarily have parked itself. Adding still further to the overall sense of endlessness is the forlorn bleat of a microwave oven attempting to alert you that the defrost cycle has run its course.

Your guests know that beep!

'My God!'

they think in collective horror,

'It isn't even *cooked* yet!'

The disquiet filling the room like a fog can be enhanced by forgetting to refill your guests' hard-won first drinks. Continue to demand an answer to your question about raindrops and remain unaware of the plaintive glances towards the liquor cabinet and the frantic swirling of naked ice cubes pleading to be reclothed.

MISANTHROPIC MEAL-MAKING

It is now time to attend to that essential element of any dinner party, even the world's worst.

Food.

And it is to the kitchen that you rush. Moments later the guests hear the quiet cursing of a frustrated chef, and simultaneously experience a horrible foreboding of the nature of the meal to come:

'Oh no . . . not again!'

or:

'Cocky's been a naughty boy!'

There is a short pause, followed by noises of another discovery —
then the sound of an aerosol spray-can being emptied to the
associated muttering of:

'Got you . . . all of you!'

Wander nonchalantly out of the kitchen, ignoring the gazes of your
dinner guests, completely stripped of optimism, their imaginations
conjuring up foul concoctions of offal, family pets and guano, and
announce in a chipper voice:

'Dinner is served.'

Although not a word has been spoken by *them*, something in your
guests' eyes suggests they have lost the faculty of speech.

Although you don't know it yet, you are about to snatch social
ignominy from the jaws of simple dinner party defeat. Because, for
the dinner itself, you will have used an iron-clad Recipe for
Disaster.

It is beyond the scope of this book to document *all* the methods of misanthropic meal-making, but suffice to say that what faces the Cookin' Fool's guests has been overcooked in the microwave, rendering the food not burnt, but utterly dehydrated. Dribbled over the top of this example of nihilist cuisine is a sauce containing an abundance of artificial sweetener, and struggling vainly against this tide of chemical gravy is something greenish, which may once have been plant life before somebody attempted to dissolve it in boiling water.

In short, the overall effect of the food on the tongues of your guests is not unlike the sensation of gargling with Oil of Cloves.

At this point the conversation suddenly heats up. Your guests, it seems, will do anything to avoid ingestion. But forge on with the pretence of etiquette. You know that the civilised host always serves wine with the meal.

Perhaps you should too.

Ignore the bottles of fine French liquor your guests have brought, leaving their Pouilly-Fuissé or Chassagne Montrachet to languish somewhere in the house, and serve instead your 'house' wine, which, it could be charitably said, has the bouquet of a septic tank and the aftertaste of a swim in the Dead Sea.

Not being quite sure what has caused your guests' faces to suddenly pucker and distort, coming to resemble the south end of a north-facing cat, you attempt to instil a vigneronic theme into the conversation, glibly uttering phrases between ghastly gulps like:

☞ 'It is an excellent quaffing white.'
☞ 'A cheeky little chardonnay!'

and:

☞ 'A delicate nose, wouldn't you agree?'

You now dovetail into the dessert course with barely a change in pace. Apologising to your guests that you are running short of plates, wash up quickly, and remark off-handedly on the origin of your tea-towels:

'Nice aren't they . . . bought them on a trip to India. Very cheap. They're recycled you see . . . from turbans.'

Now, you cannot hope to master *all* the skills of an experienced Cookin' Fool right off the bat. But with dedication and just a little luck, you can pull off a remarkably bad dinner party in no time at all. You can then move on to the next vital step of social pariahdom. Alienating yourself at *someone else's* dinner party!

In this area, as with most, there are specialists in their field. So let us look at another sub-species of social cripple.

The Party Pest :
How to Become Social Cripple Type 2

By and large the Party Pest tends to utilise the tactics of the Cookin' Fool: eg demanding customised cocktails — the 'Thrusting Manhood', or the 'Black Lagoon' — regularly and loudly. And, like any good Social Cripple, you are also a maestro of mind-numbing conversation with dinner companions:

'Lovely emerald, Mary. That reminds me, did you know they now have an emerald-based 16 kilobyte microchip capable of generating over a thousand binary characters per second at a baud rate of 2400? I mean *what* do you think of that?'

But the primary talent of a Party Pest is your singular expertise at hanging around the kitchen and annoying the cook. The basic steps are listed in the guide opposite.

Whether, in your quest to become a Social Cripple, you choose the tactic of the culinary hijack or prefer to torpedo your own dinner party, remember, if your friends are true they will forgive you anything.

So try harder!

Step-by-step Guide to Infuriating the Cook

1. Rummage in a cutlery drawer for a spoon to stir the cook's sauce with, taste it, then withdraw your finger from the sauce and say: 'More salt don't you think?'

2. Adjust the oven temperature. Exclaim: 'Twenty degrees lower makes all the difference!' but fail to identify the nature of the difference.

3. Wander around the kitchen in a blasé fashion before allowing your eyes to fall upon a can next to the sink. Cry: '*Tinned* tomatoes?' probing the cook's psyche for a deep personal confession.

4. Pull a piece of pasta from a bubbling pot, chew it and murmur: 'Post *al dente.*'

5. Strenuously offer to help serve the meal, and as you hand out the plates, comment to your dinner party companions:

'Try it — I'd be curious to know what you think.'
and:
'I suppose veal just wasn't available.'
and:
'You may need to add some salt.'

before making a small joke out of how the host has arranged the cutlery: 'Big fork on the *outside*, Derek!'

6. Proceed to re-set the table, before sitting down, reaching ostentatiously for the salt, and remarking: 'Can anyone guess whether the tomatoes are real or not?'

Creative Self-abasement

Chapter 4

So far in this book we have studied the art of disgusting and repelling small groups of familiar people — colleagues at work, dinner guests, perhaps the neighbourhood mailman or paperboy. Now it is time to learn what those in the business of failure call 'Creative Self-abasement' — embarrassing yourself in front of complete strangers.

The motto for this chapter?

'It is not important if you are disliked just because of who you happen to be. It is essential!'

The Appearance Psychopath:

How to Become Self-abaser Type 1

The Appearance Psychopath is pound for pound the most energy efficient form of Self-abaser there is. Your talent lies in not actually having to speak, but rather succeeding in repelling those around you simply by *being*.

You are conscious that the eyes of the world are on you every time you venture into public.

Apart from obsessively brushing imaginary lint off your clothes as you stand upright in a crowded commuter bus, an Appearance Psychopath's first major concern is hair control.

Repeatedly slap the top of your head in the bus, convinced that some freak static electricity storm or sunspot has caused your hair to rise and dance about like an Indian genie. Next, run your fingernails through your eyebrows to check they are not poking out at odd angles. But remember — one action has not replaced the other; they must occur simultaneously.

As your fellow commuters edge away to give you more room for self-examination, move on to that part of your morning routine given over to oral hygiene. You are *positive* your breath would knock out a goat at twenty paces. Therefore, in addition to head slapping and eyebrow adjusting, avail yourself of a variety of dental products — toothpicks, mouth-sprays — finally deciding that a good flossing will cure the problem and render you publicly acceptable again. But there is more.

You now enter the psychological state known as 'Personal Hygiene Dementia'.

First, scour your ears using a variety of implements depending on the required depth: cotton buds, discarded matches, ballpoint pen caps. Then triple-check your fingernails, holding them up to the light to assure yourself that they are spotless. Then perform a couple more complete rounds of the above actions, before realising . . .

Oh God!

How could this have happened!

Oh no!

A nostril hair!

OH GOD!

A nostril hair which, like the weed that it is, has grown out of the dark towards the sun. A nostril hair which *must* have been obvious for the entire journey.

How horrible! How degrading . . .

'*No wonder people have been looking at me!*'

you think dismally.

All is lost!

You remember that golden rule of appearance perfection . . .

'When in doubt, rip it out!'

. . . too late.

We now move on to another form of Self-abaser, one only slightly less efficient than the Appearance Psychopath. Rather than standing still, this type must ambulate. We are of course referring to . . .

The Footpath Impediment:
How to Become Self-abaser Type 2

The Footpath Impediment is proficient in the art of provocative perambulation. As the title suggests, it is the self-appointed mission of the Footpath Impediment to impede. You impede almost exclusively during peak-hour footpath use, tripping up, slowing down, bumping into and halting altogether, hundreds — sometimes thousands — of fellow pedestrians.

THE ELECTRONICALLY-INSPIRED IMPEDIMENT

A recent invention has greatly enhanced the ability of the Footpath Impediment to unconsciously frustrate an already maddened crowd — the inaptly named Sony 'Walkman'. Here's how to utilise the 'Walkman' approach:

Have your 'walkman' hidden in some bodily orifice, its cable sneaking out towards your ears and into a set of firmly attached headphones.

The actual sound you choose to have coursing up that cable is irrelevant, as long as the effect produced on you, the Footpath Impediment, is dramatic. Amidst a crowd of people who can hear nothing save the usual hub-bub of the city, you twitch violently to a primitive rhythm, shaking your head frantically. Occasionally shout something which is definitely not musical in origin but which could be:

'Oh baby! Oh, oh, baby! Yeah!'

So overwhelming is the din ricocheting through your skull, that you have no perception of fellow pedestrians, and make your way through them twitching, shouting and shaking your head as if they do not exist.

The view from above is not unlike an enraged Zulu warrior dancing through a large flock of sheep.

THE GRAND PRIX PERAMBULATOR

This Ayrton Senna of the sidewalk believes everything in life is a competition, even getting to the other side of the street first, or catching the 'Don't Walk' signal while it is still flashing.

You are Master of the Footpath, always ahead of your designated competitors — carefully using oncoming pedestrians as a shield to frustrate anyone trying to pass you. The Fangio Footpath Impediment overtakes, blocks and tails other pedestrians as if you and they are in cars.

Which they aren't.

Which means you and lots of other people often get hurt.

Which means you are hated and often have your shins kicked in during rare stationary moments — which occur only when it is a choice between having your shins kicked in or having your head transformed into a hood ornament on an oncoming cement truck.

THE ESCALATOR LOUNGER

As this particular form of interior blockage you hurry everywhere, except when you get onto an escalator. Once positioned you forget you possess functioning legs. You arrange a multitude of shopping bags in a methodical fashion to block anyone trying to get past. Or simply adopt the lateral approach and lean across the escalator. You can achieve particularly high levels of irritation in airports — on those long flat escalators called moving footways, which can be the difference between making and missing a flight. Build a veritable mountain of luggage across the moving footway, lie on top of it and leer at delayed travellers as they are forced to a complete stop and collapse, still pleading, under the continued momentum of their suitcases.

THE UNPREDICTABLE IMPEDIMENT

As this type you invent silly personal walking games which you insist on playing *only* when in a dense crowd, like not stepping on the cracks, or avoiding manhole covers, or stepping on every second crack and hopping over manhole covers. Or leaping over cracks in the pike position with a twist, and triple somersaulting over manhole covers! This technique can make you the most successful Footpath Impediment of them all, because you are utterly unpredictable and any fellow pedestrian who tries to work out the insect pattern of your movements usually ends up walking into a street sign.

So far we have looked primarily at non-verbal Self-abasers. Now we move on to the walking *and* talking variety. Inevitably this examination will involve a reprise of the art of mind-numbing conversation (see previous chapter) but used in a new and different way: **with complete strangers!** Let us meet . . .

The Soiree Sisyphus:
How to Become Self-abaser Type 3

The Soiree Sisyphus is the conversational equivalent of the mythological Greek failure after whom you are named (Sisyphus' idea of a career path was rolling a large rock up an even larger hill — forever!)

You are the career diplomat who turns up at the Anarchist's Ball and attempts to befriend people. You are the philatelist who attempts to find common ground with a drunken football crowd.

You are the embalmer at a kindergarten party.

You are, at your most developed, the Soiree Sisyphus — the would-be bon vivant whose life's failure owes much to your matchless incapacity to mix with other people.

A Soiree Sisyphus can be found at any social gathering — a party or barbecue, possibly even a wedding or a funeral. In any case you are in the company of a group of complete strangers, either because no-one is prepared to admit knowing you, or because you gatecrashed. Perhaps you saw a barbecue going on in a park and simply walked up for a steak; or maybe you were coming back from the video store with *Return of the Living Dead*, spotted a wake going on, and decided to join in.

In any case you are standing with people who don't know you, but who have no reason at all to *dislike* you. You are about to change all that.

Quickly.

The group you are trying to ingratiate yourself with consists of about six people, of mixed sex, engaged in deep conversation. Listening earnestly to them, you decide to speak.

You cough to draw attention to yourself. Unfortunately something gets caught in your throat and your delicate 'ahem' becomes a bubbling, hacking wheeze that sounds potentially life threatening.

But the group, assuming that you must have some reason for existence, looks at you expectantly, in the hope that you will add something to their lives apart from the vague sense of nausea you are currently contributing.

You are about to let them down.

Heavily.

THE NON-TOPIC OF CONVERSATION

In such moments of crisis, in the suddenness of having to be interesting, a Soiree Sisyphus has a sixth sense about the topic to be chosen. The subject of your opening conversation should be without fail something your audience has absolutely no knowledge of.

Due to a profound lack of interest.

But more importantly, it should become obvious as soon as your words can be heard between your wheezing that you have no idea what you are talking about either.

Which presents a small problem with regard to the onward flow of conviviality.

You speak excitedly, but unconvincingly, for a few minutes on the facts surrounding Ghana being the first West African country to have direct-dial telephones. The group observes your excitement curiously and fails utterly to respond to it. You finish speaking.

The group allows a moment of silence to pass, as if to emphasise to anyone else who may have been listening that your afro-telephonic monologue had nothing to do with them.

Then the group picks up where they left off.

UTILISING THE UNIVERSALLY APPLICABLE PHRASE

You now shift gear and decide that, rather than initiate new topics, you will grab the conversational ball and run with it.

Your first step is tentative, feeling out the conversation and its participants. Not wanting to say the wrong thing, you say only one thing — your favourite Universally Applicable Phrase.

For the next ten minutes you utter only this phrase — but utter it with conviction:

Unfolding Conversation: '. . . and so that's how I got into advertising in the first place.'

Soiree Sisyphus: 'I bet that was a whole new ball of wax!'

Unfolding Conversation: '. . . isn't it incredible about the election result?'

Soiree Sisyphus: 'Yes — it's a whole new ball of wax now!'

Unfolding Conversation: '. . . unbelievable what medicine can do, things are changing so fast . . . I read where they can now transplant ears!'

Soiree Sisyphus: 'Yep. It's a whole new ball of wax these days!'

You now begin to determine the professions of your fellow bon-vivants. This knowledge allows you further access to the conversation:

'Yes, well a teacher would say that . . .'

and:

'I know how this must look to a doctor, but to the rest of us . . .'

and:

'You truly believe that? . . . What do you do again?'

THE GRATUITOUS ASSERTION AND MOVING TO THE HIGH MORAL GROUND

Pumped up now, certain you are the centre of the group's collective interest, you imbibe another cocktail and exhibit perhaps your finest talent in the field of mind-numbing conversation. The ability to make gratuitous assertions which do not add a single thing to the conversation:

'Ah, you are one of those who still believes that.'

and:

'I used to think that when I was your age too.'

and:

'I've heard that argument put unsuccessfully before.'

Then, as though you are tiring of the small talk going on around you, swallow your gin deeply and move the conversation on to the high moral ground:

'I know we're having fun but I think we should consider what the Kurdish people are going through right now.'

You then boast that you are supporting a family in Ethiopia for $2.50 a month. When someone else in the group says they are supporting a family in India for only $2 a month, say dismissively:

'The cost of living is higher in Ethiopia!'

And finally, suffering in part from an alcohol-induced delusion that anything you say is not only interesting, but wise and witty at the same time (as well as thoughtful and intelligent), deliver your final round of repartee — let loose a few party-paralysing unprovoked profundities, like:

'If everyone on Earth stopped talking right now, what do you imagine we would hear?'

and then:

'What do you think the chances are of someone in the world being murdered in the next two seconds?'

followed by:

'It's an interesting thought, isn't it? That in the time we've been talking someone we know may have died.'

and finally:

'Who knows? Maybe one of us will be attacked and murdered after we leave the party.'

As you totter off into the night, you can also perform many of the rituals of your fellow Self-abasers, the Footpath Impediment and the Appearance Psychopath, and become, briefly, that lowest form of Fast-track Failure . . .

The Trinity of Torpidity!

Becoming an Object of Ridicule

Chapter 5

The opportunities open to the perceptive failure are so many that it is beyond the scope of this book to deal with all of them — however, some key inspirational pursuits are listed below under the general heading 'Becoming an Object of Ridicule'. But please — do not limit yourself to these —

> *R*emember, as a bright young failure, the world is your bad oyster.

You can, with the correct training and by wasting enough money on books like this, become an Object of Ridicule over such a broad spectrum of social interaction that it will be the job description you put on your tax form.

Here, then, are a few sample life areas to set you on the path to becoming the village idiot.

The Tortuous Traveller:
How to Become Object
of Ridicule Type 1

There are few people more universally despised outside their homes than the Tortuous Traveller. The one person you never want to get on a plane, ship or train with. Travel, by its very nature, throws people together who would not ordinarily choose to be together — in fact who would probably, as a matter of personal hygiene, normally try to stay as far from each other as possible.

Yes, it is an extraordinarily loathsome feat being a traveller who makes fellow travellers pray for a derailment, an iceberg, or a mid-air collision, rather than continue talking to him.

In fact there is more than one airline currently discussing a special 'infrequent fliers program', whereby the more such a Traveller from Hell stays off their planes, the more free gifts he can win.

While on the subject of air travel, let us take the Awful Air Traveller as our specific example of this sub-class of failure.

There are many types of Awful Air Travellers who are tolerable because there's not a damn thing they can do about their problem. These include chronic fondlers of air-sick bags, two year olds, and people who nurse deep phobias about air travel (like a morbid fear that Puff the Magic Dragon will collide with a wing and send them all hurtling earthward to a final, ghastly inferno).

However, there is a Mr Big of Truly Awful Air Travellers. He is the yardstick by which all others are judged. Consider the following case study.

CASE STUDY A

As Mr Big steps onto the plane he immediately gives the impression that he is somehow different, somehow bigger, than all the other passengers. **'HANG THIS!'** he says dismissively to a smaller passenger, giving him his coat.

Then Mr Big takes his window seat, chosen specifically, it seems, because the window is the exact shape of his enormous head and not a scrap of light escapes past it when he presses it up against the glass — so that the short passenger next to him is left with the sensation that he is sitting in a large gun barrel.

As the plane climbs from the ground, Mr Big informs the seven dwarfs within earshot that most major air disasters occur in the first two minutes after take-off. The plane jolts as it passes through a windshear and hearing the gasp from the diminutive creature next to him, Mr Big turns and sneers **'TURBULENCE!'**, as if he enjoys the sensation of falling out of the sky to certain death.

Bellowing peals of huge laughter, the force of which flattens his immediate circle of lesser beings like grass in a wind storm, Mr Big almost misses the bar service.

'A Bloody Mary, light on the tomato juice, heavy on the tabasco! And leave an extra vodka, tomato juice, the pepper and salt containers, and a few sticks of celery so I can mix another!' he says, glancing at himself to direct the stewardess's eyes towards his bigness. 'And a couple more packets of nuts — there's a good little girl!' Mr Big then spreads the makings of his Bloody Mary all over his tray table and the one belonging to Noddie on his right, who is forced to nurse his drink on his knee and watch it splash on to his trousers.

If Mr Big is travelling in First Class, he stands at the curtain separating First from Economy, holding his drink and usually a complex canape, and stares disdainfully at those on the other side of the drape. He occasionally taunts them by ordering 'more smoked salmon'.

Mr Big then plugs his headphones into the comedy channel and prods his physically deficient neighbour as each joke is told, urging him to laugh as well — even though the latter is actually listening to classical music. Then Mr Big tires of the comedy and switches to the 'Beautiful Music' channel, singing along with Val Doonican and Barry Manilow, out loud. The effect is as if he is trying to hum 'Ride of the Valkyries' as it sounds played on a two-stroke lawn mower.

Mr Big's aural torture of the pygmy passengers continues until the meal service, by which stage everyone on the plane has made separate pacts with themselves that if they ever meet Barry Manilow or Val Doonican they will summarily tear their tongues out.

'The chicken or the steak sir?' asks the stewardess. **'TWO STEAKS!'** replies Mr Big expansively.

As he eats, Mr Big talks down to the midget who has his chicken meal balanced perilously on his lap, spraying him with pieces of steak as he does so. On the few occasions he asks the gnome a question, Mr Big times it to when his quivering neighbour has just filled his mouth and then asks something like: 'So you were born and then what happened?' As the petrified pipsqueak struggles to swallow and begins to reply, Mr Big, making it obvious he expected a short reply, exclaims: **'IN TWENTY WORDS OR LESS!'**

After the meal, Mr Big removes a large toiletries pack the size of a suitcase from the overhead locker and stands in the queue for the bathroom, mentioning to the hobbits behind him that he always likes to have a full body wash and shampoo after a meal. Once in the bathroom, he flushes the toilet every ten minutes or so to give those waiting false hope. He chuckles as he finally walks out to see the effect on his fellow travellers, who seem to be engaged in some strange sort of Lilliputian folk dance — hands in pockets, knees gripped tightly together and lips pursed — as they walk about in circles.

Finally, our Traveller from the Dark Side seems to have only one mode of transport once the plane has landed: the sort advertised by very small men holding very large signs which read:

'WELCOME CORPORATE WUNDERKIND!'

The Lumpenshopper:
How to Become Object
of Ridicule Type 2

When discussing abject failure and public ridicule in the context of shopping, one must first make the distinction between the 'shopper' and the 'salesperson'. The difference is this.

> **The 'salesperson' is one who has had extensive instruction and intense hands-on training to learn how to maximise the misery and discomfort he or she can inflict on those who walk into their shop, whereas the 'shopper' is a rank amateur at the same.**

There are many tricks one can learn, though, in the quest to become the Shopper from the Black Lagoon. You can, for example, practise the 'Reverse Ambulation' technique by pushing your trolley the wrong way around the supermarket. Or you can adopt the 'Maginot Line' defence of double parking your trolley to halt the collective onward advance of every shopper in the supermarket.

This can cause great distress to any phobic shopper present who suffers from a brooding anxiety that one day she will be surrounded by supermarket trolleys and have lettuces thrown at her.

Then there is the 'Misanthropic Marketer' — sighing, grunting and growling at all those who dare slow his escape route to the checkout. This horror-shopper behaves as if he was last in the supermarket before it was open to the public and is furious to actually find people cluttering up the aisles!

Finally, of course, there is the common or garden collection of failure shoppers, whose original thinking for misery-enhancement runs only as far as choosing the wrong checkout queue.

But there is one superior genus of Lumpenshopper, clearly the most successful in existence. The one masquerading as a sweet little old lady! Read and learn.

Case Study B

TROLLEY TREACHERY

I t is busy (it always is!) and there are no trolleys. Watch as the Sweet Little Old Lady adopts the *'Thinking Deeply And Exclusively About The Great-grandkids'* demeanour coupled with the *'What Is This Big Place And How Did I Get Here?'* expression as she deftly walks away with a trolley whose owner has left it momentarily to pick up an extra tub of yoghurt. With a skill which comes from having lifted more trolleys than you and I have had great-grandkids, the Sweet Little Old Lady quickly discards the current contents of her trolley onto inappropriate shelves (cat food in the spaghetti section, dog biscuits behind the Iced Vo-vos etc).

Or she simply dumps the goods in someone else's trolley.

At this point we flit ahead to view the effects of this Lumpenshopping on other shoppers who have reached the checkout.

Victim 1 of our Sweet Little Old Lady is currently muttering:

'Aisle crawling deviants!'

as he develops an instant and intense hatred for the unknown person or persons who spiked the tinned spaghetti section with cans of cat food, and put dog biscuits behind the Iced Vo-vos. Even, fumes the Lumpenvictim to himself, if it was not a malicious act — simply someone who got as far as aisle seven before remembering they didn't have either a cat or dog — it hardly matters now as he now finds himself on the wrong side of the cash register with three tins of spaghetti, a can of My Cat and a packet of Iced Vo-vos, nestled next to a bag of Puppy Nibbles.

Our Lumpenvictim now informs the disbelieving sixteen year old behind the cash register that he doesn't own a cat or dog, and asks if she could please perform some mathematical gymnastics with his total? Added to this ignominy is the Greek chorus behind him in the queue, murmuring nasty murmurs about his parentage and suggesting mean-spirited suggestions about the sort of dog he should own and what it should be fed on. Finally the Lumpenvictim whirls around from his hopeless conversation with the checkout girl (who never did maths) and explains to the rest of the queue that someone, or possibly a group of people acting together, have spiked the spaghetti section.

There is silence.

Then someone from the back of the queue shouts:

'AND ELVIS IS WORKING IN THE DELICATESSEN!'

Meanwhile, our Sweet Little Old Lady is giving full rein to the Lumpentalent which most maddens her fellow shoppers.

GROCERY TOUCHING

There are sub-species of Lumpenshoppers who fill the ranks of the Cheese Squeezers, Margarine Openers, Milk Returners, Bread Grabbers and Biscuit Crumblers — but we are in luck. Our Sweet Little Old Lady is a Fruit Feeler!

The Fruit Feeler has a deep and unquenchable need to fondle articles of vegetation. There are specialist Celery Benders, Melon Shakers, Carrot Twisters, Potato Scrapers, Lettuce Examiners, Avocado Squeezers, Grape Stealers, Onion Rustlers, Bean Snappers and Corn Strippers.

Our Sweet Little Old Lady, though, is a human salad bowl of desires. She walks through the fruit section prodding, poking and replacing (most often in the wrong place). And the beauty of it is that no-one attempts to stop her. One shopper frowns severely at the Lumpenshopper as she prods her fourth peach and pokes her third apple. The Sweet Little Old Lady looks at the enraged

shopper amiably, squeezes the apple one last time for good measure
and says: 'Fruit's not what it used to be, is it?'

And how does the fellow who observes the Sweet Little Old Lady
hanging around the root-vegetables section vent his frustration?
He's not going to be the one to walk up to a Sweet Little Old Lady
in a public place and shout:

'STOP STROKING THAT CARROT!',

quite simply because he knows if he does he will be arrested, sent
to gaol and once there, unspeakable things will happen to him.

The time has now come for our Sweet Little Old Lady to perform
the act which has made her famous in the field of Lumpenshopping.

The 'Oblivious' Queue Jump

Holding two apples, she totters into a gap which has just opened
up in the front end of a queue which stretches back to the dairy
section. She has calculated her approach and timed her entry to
perfection.

'Oi!'

says the 18 stone truck driver who has just realised that the cash
register is further away by the distance of one Sweet Little Old
Lady. Shaking himself for a moment at the strain of such a complex
realisation, the truck driver speaks again:

'Oi!'

'Oh, I'm sorry sonny, I didn't see you,' says our consummate
Lumpenshopper, 'well I only have these two apples . . . I'm sure
you won't mind . . . such a nice young man.'

But the truck driver, who has been reliably informed that he is the
product of a laboratory experiment, is utterly lacking in filial instinct
and moves forward to forcibly eject the Sweet Little Old Lady from
the queue.

She responds as the pro she is, wearing an expression which says: *'I'm not at my best when I'm vertical and I could be a lot of trouble to you if I don't get through the checkout quickly and home to my pills.'*

Then she swoons against the chewing gum rack.

That is enough for the Mack-mover. The last thing he needs is a bunch of ambulances blocking up *his* roads, so he grunts and lets the Sweet Little Old Lady in.

Her face now wears the simultaneous expressions of *'Thank You Young Man'* and a brief reprise of *'What Is This Big Place And How Did I Get Here?'* as she pulls in the trolley load she had shunted in next to the magazines while she waited for her soft-touch target in the queue.

But our master Lumpenshopper has one last hurdle to trip over, one final barb to toss at the unsuspecting.

THE ALL-STOPS CHECKOUT

An ersatz (or would-be) Madonna checkout chick, with a mouth full of chewing gum, waits at her station. She believes that sitting behind a cash register is close to the most powerful position in the Western world.

'This is an express checkout!' barks the curt sixteen-year-old voice, redolent with pubescent authority, at the aged Lumpenshopper. She repeats this phrase with lessening degrees of pubescent authority as the Sweet Little Old Lady — showing not a scrap of awareness that the checkout girl exists — merrily piles her trolley load onto the counter, oblivious of the final, weak: ' . . . this is an . . . express . . . checkout . . .' delivered by the defeated checkout girl before she begins punching keys.

And as a final *coup de grace* the Sweet Little Old Lady reaches into her pile of shopping just as the checkout girl punches up the total, and pulls out an item, asking:

'How much is it if you take away this?'

Lumpenshopper 1. Remainder of Supermarket Population 0.

Do not let age, gender or physical characteristics deter you when attempting to follow the role model above. For trying this technique before you have reached the age of about 105 and have heard all the jeers and insults the world has to offer is guaranteed to make your life abjectly miserable. However, be warned. Trying to be a Lumpenshopper if you are small, male, and between the ages of seventeen and thirty-five may be a serious health hazard — for there are few animals on Earth as vicious as the enraged super-market shopper.

The Unneighbour:
How to Become Object of Ridicule Type 3

The brotherhood of man, the common destiny, the love of kind . . . all well and good but not on *your* street!

The art of becoming unneighbourly is possibly the easiest talent to learn in the search for the bottom line of one's personality.

An Unneighbour begins by training his children to harass co-dwellers of the street.

YOUR PROVOCATIVE PROGENY

Kids are the 'air war' of unneighbourliness, the first strike of the sub-suburbanite. These runt grunts can begin with strafing runs of your neighbour's house, raining various projectiles incessantly on his walls, windows and lawn — balls, rocks, small animals, dead birds etc . . . in an effort to loosen up his defences for the frontal assault by you, the Unneighbour.

But any good war requires good intelligence. An Unneighbour realises this, and apart from restricting your *neighbour's* intelligence by rising at 4.00 am to steal his home-delivered newspaper every morning, and scattering small rocks on his lawn in the hope that one will hit his head when he's mowing, you also send your children to spy on him.

Under the guise of retrieving their various projectiles or animals, these dwarf detectives and midget Mata Haris can be utilised to seek out the important information you need for your campaign of terror. Information you can use to embarrass your neighbour in public places like:

☞ his brand of aftershave;

☞ the colour of his wife's pyjamas;

☞ whether he is weak and succumbed to the door-to-door encyclopedia salesperson;

☞ the titles of any X-rated videos he might have kicking around the house;

☞ the colour of *his* pyjamas and whether they have anything silly written on them like 'Hot Stuff' or 'Big Boy' (the invariable informational target of the Sunday morning spy run);

☞ and whether he is planning to get any interesting magazines delivered with the newspapers.

As well as being secret agents, your team of reconnaissance rug-rats can also be ankle-biting *agents provocateurs*, charged with infecting your neighbour's children with the virus of greed.

Listen to them with pride as they diligently dash about your neighbour's house, mouthing words guaranteed to turn his children against him:

'My daddy's going to buy me a jet-ski for my birthday!'
'Oh yeah!'

reply his unwitting progeny:

'Then *my* daddy's going to buy me a jet-ski too!'

And as your neighbour attempts to explain to his children that his name is Jones and not Onassis, your eyes and ears are already halfway up the stairs to his bedroom to try one last time to find that pair of pyjamas his wife gave him as a joke last Valentine's Day.

CHEMICAL WEAPONRY

After the small-arms attack, you launch your chemical weapons. The source of your noxious fumes is either a diabolical brand of barbecue marinade or a couple of well-placed plastic items in your incinerator. Most often you choose the timing of your offensive gas offensives to coincide with high level outdoor meetings between your neighbour and his allies (ie lunches) in an effort to leave him diplomatically isolated and vulnerable.

D-DAY

Your major assault is heralded by battle cries from your beasts (which, anticipating a long campaign, possibly even a siege, have ploughed your neighbour's vegetable patch back into the earth in an attempt to starve him out).

As dawn on D-day nears, the dog howling, caterwauling and budgie chirruping reach a crescendo.

In the hour before the offensive your neighbour's newspaper disappears almost as soon as it hits his lawn.

You know that to win you must first seize control of the press.

Then finally you launch yourself into the fray. It is the moment you have been waiting for, the chance to do it man-to-man! Have it out! Battle to the death!

SUNDAY BLOODY SUNDAY!

Your neighbour walks, seemingly casually, toward you, but you know the war cry resounding in his head:

'No more rocks on the lawn!!!'

You know you have the upper hand; your pipsqueak hit squad and mustard-gas-marinade have brought him to a state of immediate pre-surrender.

He stares at you with a steely glint, edged with tungsten and finished off with diamond dust and some really nasty looking spikes.

You meet his stare and raise it.

Neither of you speak, though the air around you is throbbing with tension and mutual abhorrence. He fires the first shot: 'Morning Smith.'

But your return volley is more powerful:

'Morning Jones.'

You glint at him for a moment more before you are satisfied that he knows the score and it is Smith 1, Jones 0 — so you accept his implicit surrender with a stern stare and check your letterbox in a he-man way which indicates that if you had chosen to you could have taken him apart limb by limb.

The Highway to Hell:
How to Become Object of <u>Ridicule</u> Type 4

Streams and streams of iron-clad failures line the road to ridicule, jostling each other and revving their engines at Life's intersections. With diligence, you, too, can drive yourself to distraction.

There are many types of Motorised Malcontent to choose from. You might be the driver who seeks to save petrol by simply parking your car on a highway, putting it in neutral and letting the Earth's rotation or continental drift do the rest — a.k.a. The Human Speed-hump. You know you will *eventually* get to where you are going. After all, India finally reached the rest of Asia didn't it?

Or you might be the Autoneurotic.

THE AUTONEUROTIC: MOTORISED MALCONTENT TYPE 1

An Autoneurotic is one who becomes neurotic the moment he steps into an automobile. From the moment the pistons start pumping, the Autoneurotic becomes very, very, very tense. Tense at everything! Other drivers, their cars, road signs, traffic lights, pedestrians . . . Especially pedestrians!

Every time something other than him ventures on or near the

road, the Autoneurotic works himself into a state of jaw-grinding, sphincter-tightening tension. About three stop signs and four pedestrians into his trip, the Autoneurotic begins rocking backwards and forwards in his seat as tension becomes anger. Five more pedestrians and one major intersection later the Autoneurotic is rocking backwards and forwards and bobbing up and down in his seat as anger becomes fury. And if this next filthy pedestrian jay-walks across his road!

'It happened!!! Do you believe that newt just did that on my road!!!' The Autoneurotic howls to himself in capital letters:

'AAAAAARRRRRRRGGGGHH!!!!'

By this stage our Autoneurotic has taken the left-hand turn in Life towards Autopsychosis. Physically he is utterly immobile, his knuckles blue on the steering wheel. But examining him a little more closely, one can see a shimmering effect just under his skin as the ripples of rage bounce uncontrollably inside his body. He is in reality a seething, bubbling mass of rage from which two arms stick out. He is physically incapable of going on. He is in what various motoring associations term 'human meltdown mode'.

Chernobyl in a Commodore!

Occasionally some primitive reflex action activates one of his legs to push the brake or accelerator and either stop him immediately or direct him into a user-friendly road sign to hold him up long enough for the proper authorities to get to him.

Unfortunately, our Autoneurotic has hit a particularly large road sign with a bad attitude which promptly hit him back.

Still, he has ended up where most Autoneurotics do — a hospital. It is just a question of which ward they occupy: emergency, intensive care, psychiatric . . . or simply the garage if no surgeon is immediately available to cut the Autoneurotic from his car.

The life of an Autoneurotic is a cyclical thing. A few minutes on the road leads to a profound fury and an urge to become Carjack the Ripper, followed by some form of rest, relaxation, and therapy. Then back on the road for . . .

THE RETURN OF CARJACK!

THE CARPHONE DWEEB: MOTORISED MALCONTENT TYPE 2

There are many other popular descriptions for this type of human highway impediment. Studies into their habits have proved the existence of a secret society of Carphone-dweebs through which carphone numbers are handed out. Part of the scientific proof for the reality of this motorised masonic club is that there is simply no other way of accounting for the vast number of calls made by Carphone-dweebs and, most importantly, no logical explanation for who they actually call!

It has been rumoured that at their secret meetings, Carphone-dweebs run competitions to hone their techniques. An insider managed to pass on the following information about these tests of skill just before she hung up forever:

---

1. Carphone-dweeb Endurance Tests:

- Longest Conversation on Car-Phone while Stationary at a Green Light.
- Longest Conversation on Car-Phone while Occupying Parking Space on Busy Street.
- Longest Conversation on Car-Phone while Ignoring Milling, Jeering Crowd on Pedestrian Crossing which Car Blocks.

2. Carphone-dweeb Speed Tests:

- Most Car-Phone calls to Home or Work while driving between Home and Work.
- Most Profanities Shouted at Other Drivers while on Car-Phone.
- Highest Speed Reached while Juggling Car-Phone.

3. Combination Carphone Events:

- Conversing on Car-Phone while in Fast Lane and Keeping Car Exactly next to Car in Slow Lane.
- Answering Important Car-Phone Call while Searching for Money at Toll Gate.
- Timing Intimate Car-Phone Call to when Scanner Freak is Recording.

Further achievements in this field will soon be possible as society slowly but inexorably drives into the age of the Car-Fax!

HOONMAN: MOTORISED MALCONTENT TYPE 3

As a Hoonman or Hoonwoman type, you have lost the faculty of speech completely and have only your car as a form of communication and self-expression. (Hoonmen are a close relative of that other walking fiasco detailed in Chapter 15 — The Pet Expressive.)

There are a number of things as a Hoonman you can do to draw attention to yourself:

☞ Paint a huge, well-endowed maiden being rescued from the back of your car by Arnold Schwarzenegger.

☞ Staple an example of the art of taxidermy to your aerial.

☞ Hang a swollen, foam-filled advertisement for your other life interest from the rear vision mirror (ie large dice, large dog, large male body parts etc).

☞ Raise the suspension of your Hoonmobile so high that you must garage your machine under a bridge in order to climb in and out.

To further become the focus of the world you pass through, Hoonmen and Hoonwomen must plaster their vehicles with bumper stickers. In socio-linguistic studies of losers and flops, it has been determined that if Hoonpeople *could* speak, their conversations would be peppered with maxims like:

☞ 'Honk if you think I'm sexy.'

☞ 'Love is a Bull Terrier.'

☞ 'Doze in a Greenie.'

☞ 'Golfers do it with small white balls.'

and

☞ 'I'd rather be whaling.'

It is often interesting for students of Applied Idiocy to study the subtle differences between Hoonpeople who exclaim 'Love is a Great Dane' and those softer, more sensitive types who proclaim their preference as 'Love is a Cocker Spaniel'. (Having tried neither, this author will not comment on the validity of either of these statements.)

The Fool at Play:
How to Become Object of Ridicule Type 5

You have, no doubt, often seen the Fool at Play. There goes one, jogging across the beach imagining he is conjuring up thoughts of *Terminator 2* in the minds of his sun-drenched audience, when in reality he is more reminiscent of *Pee Wee's Big Adventure* due to his unfortunate jogging style which looks like a two year old girl playing hopscotch with both arms tied to her dress at the elbows.

There goes another Fool — already in the surf! In his mind he is forging through the water like Mark Spitz but the public effect is quite different, as his swimming technique suggests:

(a) A clockwork bath toy winding down.
(b) A seal missing a flipper.
or:
(c) Someone who has just fallen into a hole in the water.

The beach is a good place to pick up the techniques of the Fool at Play: the idiot diving spectacularly but fruitlessly for a volleyball; the clown who rides a surfboard as though it has a built in squat-toilet; or the sunbaker who, simply by his method of lying on his stomach, comes to resemble beach debris. But the beach is not the only playground for Fools.

There is also the tennis court. This venue rivals the beach in its potential to showcase the truly ludicrous sportsperson, and provide a focus for public scorn and derision.

Case Study C

Let us look at our Not-Newcombe and our Less-than-Lendl at play. The first resembles a ballet dancer struggling through an epileptic fit; the second seems to think he is playing soccer — running backwards and forward to the net waving his arms, without reference to the ball's position.

Further along we sight an impaired pair playing mixed doubles with a twist: the 'twist' being that the object of this Fool's sport seems to be mistaking one's partner's head for the ball.

Back to our first Fools. Not-Newcombe is interspersing his missed shots with phrases like:

☞ 'Next time Ivan!'

☞ 'I'm better on grass!'

☞ 'Forehand is my natural game!'

☞ 'Since they developed these new racquets, the sport's gone right out if it!'

And when his rancid racquetry actually pulls off a return of serve he roars triumphantly:

☞ **'POWERPLAY!'**

The Tennis Fool further draws attention to the paucity of his game by arguing McEnroe-fashion with the umpire.

Even though the umpire is his opponent's wife.

He screams and throws a tantrum over a disputed line call and finally hurls his racquet at the ground (from which it unfortunately bounces back to strike him and render him briefly unconscious). He argues against his service faults as though the aim of the *truly* good player is to get the ball *into* the net.

However, the true measure of a convinced Tennis Fool is the duration of his sulk after the game, regardless of the fact that he is often wearing his opponent's racquet as a form of headgear.

There are countless sports in which the Fool can choose to exhibit that, despite his obvious lack of coordinated motor functioning, he can still, somehow, manage to get by: from bowls to golf, from wrestling to chess — some actually become quite good in their chosen sports field.

Some Fools actually achieve greatness in their sport.

But they still look silly doing it.

The Horrifying Hobbyist:

How to Become Object of Ridicule Type 6

The last category in this section on becoming the village idiot is the pursuit of Horrifying Hobbies.

Horrifying Hobbyists are not horrifying as people. Their nomenclature is due to the fact that it says something horrifying about society that it can throw up people who actually *like* watching aeroplanes take off and land; or trains arrive and depart; or who like to stick used stamps, that anyone might have licked, into books; or turn good wholesome lumps of clay into vases so awful they make flowers wilt. People whose particular pastime of choice is insanely boring to the rest of humanity.

For unlike the Fool at Play, the Horrifying Hobbyist would not receive an iota of the contempt which comes his way if he simply *didn't talk about it*!

DISCUSSING YOUR HOBBY — AGAIN!

But no! As a determined Horrifying Hobbyist you believe that your dinner companions *need* to know about the types of diseases which can be caught from licking the backs of your West African stamp collection; or your fellow commuters have been waiting for the time that someone would explain to them the exciting differences between the 1966 and the 1967 one rouble coin; or why your work colleagues have all failed in *their* efforts to make a working model of a steam engine constructed only from dental floss and toothpicks.

Discussion of this last hobby usually provokes a question which lurks in the minds of listeners for years:

'Used or un-used?'

Some outstanding Fast-track Failures take up hobbies simply so they can inflict the tedium of it on others. Is there any other reason for palm plaiting, eel fishing, collecting fridge magnets, copying the Bible on to drink coasters or burying time-capsules so some future unfortunate can be depressed at what a worthless life someone once led?

WORLD RECORD RIDICULE

The other main group of Horrifying Hobbyists are those obsessed with getting their name into the *Guinness Book of Records*.

You petition the Guinness company so persistently to get your particular sideline recognised as a pursuit worthy of world record status that the good makers of the dark stuff are driven to drink large quantities of their own product. Finally though, the tenacity of the ridiculous would-be record-holder overwhelms the volume of laughter heard around the corridors of Guinness whenever the subject is raised.

Hence entries for world records like:

'Longest consistent hours operating a blender.'

'Highest altitude at which "This Land is Your Land" has been sung at.'

'Longest period of time spent immobile while covered with silkworms.'

and even:

'Most verses of "Click Go The Shears" whistled while balancing on a child's scooter.'

Once you have achieved your goal in one totally fruitless area or another you can rest on your laurels for the rest of your life, only returning to the cut and thrust of the world record scene when some other pseudo-athlete advances humankind another notch by operating a blender for three days, two hours and fifty seconds, or singing 'This Land is Your Land' in the toilet on the Concorde.

There has been more than one suggestion to mount a counter competition to the Olympic Games where all these important pursuits could be opened to international competition and even run as team events. One wonders how the person now known only by a small entry in a book of records would be feted by his fellow countrymen if he returned in triumph holding aloft the gold medal for souvenir snowstorm shaking!

If this chapter has been rather lengthy it is because there are just so *many* opportunities for a Fast-track Failure to add 'Object of Ridicule' to your list of under-achievements. Just remember — any time you are in public, chances are there is something you can do to be laughed at.

Just be yourself!

Part III

Failure in Love and Marriage

Doomed Dating and Loathsome Lovers

Chapter 6

It is pretty hard to succeed at love if every other life area you have touched has turned sour. But love is a perfect way of inflicting your misery on someone else, so give it a bash!

The first symptoms which indicate love may be happening are not unlike prickly heat. Once you are sure you are not in fact suffering from prickly heat and are in fact afflicted by love, use the following Loathsome Lover types as role models.

The Fantasiser:
How to Become
Loathsome Lover Type 1

The unfortunate thing about this type of lover is that he is the only person in love, and the object of his ardour not only doesn't love him, but often despises the ground he walks on. Still, the Fantasiser will battle on in his unrequited quest for bliss, reading into the most mundane act of his beloved a secret message for him . . . The way she pushed that outlet tap on the water cooler at work, or the way she wrapped her false nails around the paper cup and lifted it to her warm, willing lips.

The Fantasiser is marvellous at timing his arrival at work to coincide with his beloved's — so they can share the lift together and he can use the opportunity to make breezy chit-chat, which gives her a glimpse of his savoir-faire, like:

'Nice lift huh?'

'Nice music huh?'

or

'Good to be at work again, isn't it?'

Oblivious to the fact that the object of his desire is giving him less attention than she gives the office stapler, the Fantasiser assumes he is an integral part of her life and casually stops by her desk about twenty times a day to pepper her with *bon mots* which seem innocent to the rest of the office, but which *she* understands because of the look in his eyes.

Swaggering in a way which could be mistaken as merely friendly by anyone but his beloved — who immediately picks up on his brooding sexuality and senses the ecstasy her life could become if she simply devoted the remainder of it to him — the Fantasiser makes the most of every opportunity. As he waltzes by in a wonderfully unconcerned kind of way, he just happens to notice that the makers of her desk calender have seen fit to inform its owner that today is Tongan Independence Day.

> The Fantasiser: 'Interesting, isn't it?' (said in that 'hold-me-and-you'll-never-regret-it' way).
>
> Object of Desire: 'What!'(said in that 'I-think-you-are-infectious' way).
>
> The Fantasiser: 'Tonga . . . I'd like to go there some time,' (conveying visions of rolling naked in the tropical surf and making her complete as a woman).
>
> Object of Desire: 'What! (conveying visions of the Spanish Inquisition).
>
> The Fantasiser: 'Ah Tonga . . . my heart weeps for thee . . .'(making it plain that she is Tonga in the context of his impromptu ballad, but nevertheless conveying technicolour images of their passion amidst the rolling waves, as they wash like entwined seaweed onto the sand, and he makes her even more complete as a woman).
>
> Object of Desire: 'I'm busy!' (gasped dismissively)

He lingers a while longer, to let her know that he understands she had to do it, or face complete breakdown of self-control right there in the office. But at that moment he knows she feels like Ingrid Bergman at the airport in Casablanca. 'We'll always have Tonga . . .' he whispers before he wafts into the office hub-bub.

'A success!' he breathes, scarcely able to believe it himself . . .

The Fashion Lover:
How to Become Loathsome Lover Type 2

The Fashion Lover can often be found in chic restaurants, discos or movie premieres. Fashion Lovers move in pairs — not because they love each other but because they 'look' right together.

Unfortunately, as a Fashion Lover you 'look' right only to your co-Fashion Lover. The following is a description of a typical pair:

HE Your suit is raw silk — all ruffles and bows. Your shirt has no buttons but must be tied around your body. Your shoes are so pointed they give the impression you must be missing the big toe on each foot. Your socks are gold lurex and always visible, as your legs twitch fashionably when you walk. You have what appears to be a herring tied to your neck, but which is in fact the latest thing in satin bow ties, and your heavily gelled hair is tied in a pigtail.

In your mind, the look you have achieved is pure Richard Gere. Women will soon be posting themselves to your address, you rejoice inwardly.

The actual effect you have created is shockingly different. You look like an idiot.

SHE You use clothes to let the true you leap forth. No quiet mousy office garb — you have been waiting all week for this. Wild, seductive, an invitation to defoliation! The make-up, all blacks and grey pastels, not forgetting the violet contact lenses. The top? Your black Elle Macpherson bra — that's enough. An impossibly short hip tube, which requires constant hitching back down over your thighs, thick black stockings nuns of the late fifteenth century would have killed for, and over-large Bata Scout black school shoes — the kind with animal prints on the soles — finishes off your ensemble. You complete the effect by walking in a way which suggests you have a chemical addiction. You are transformed from Wendy the water cooler waif to Elvira, queen of the night!

Unfortunately, you, too, look like an idiot.

Once inside the gathering place for fashion lovers **HE** is almost strangled by his satin herring as the maitre'd pulls at what he thinks is a jacket collar.

SHE realises that her hip tube functions as a dress only when she is standing. When she sits it becomes a belt.

In conversation with each other, Fashion Lovers stoke the bonfire of inanities. Your conversations contain a preponderance of 'Oooooohs!' and 'Aaaaaaahs!' and 'Absoloooootely'. You are Vowel Treasurers, never letting one pass your lips without being magnified:

'Oooooooooh daaaaaaaaaaaarling, absolooooooooootely!'

And after a long evening of concentrated staring, vowel uttering, and occasional imitations of a blender on the dance floor, Fashion Lovers are tired but complete as individuals. You promise to meet for Sunday brunch in combined purple and olive linen.

You whisper the internationally accepted farewell of Fashion Lovers:

'Loooove the outfit!'

The Power Lover:
How to Become
Loathsome Lover Type 3

'Tuesday 7.00 pm — 11.00 pm: *Love with Jones from Accounts.*
Wednesday 6.30 am: *Power breakfast with Jones from Accounts.*
Wednesday 8.00 am: *Meeting with assistant vice-president's assistant . . . PS — re Wed. 7.00 pm app: remind Jones to bring protection . . .'*

So runs the diary of the female Power Lover.

She is impatient when Jones is late for dinner and promptly orders for both of them. She takes charge — ensuring the waiters fully grasp that she is paying good money and expects to be treated as something other than an object of ridicule. The waiters apologise and ask politely what she would like to be treated as, before she dismisses them. She turns her attention back to Jones and talks at him between courses about how the assistant vice-president's assistant is incompetent and really shouldn't be doing the job.

Then home to her place, into the sack and the night reaches its conclusion shortly before 11.00 pm to the sound of her gasping:

'G-spot you idiot! G-spot!'

The sort of male who finds himself entwined with a Power Lover generally subscribes to the following: equal time in conversation; an acute awareness of transmissible diseases; an ideologically sound music collection; and a list of restaurants which have never served whale meat.

Love and the Art of Abominable Conversation

In love or out of it, there is no greater skill in the Loathsome Lover's armory than truly rancid repartee, and crushingly corny chit-chat. The art of abominable (or mind-numbing) conversation is explained more fully elsewhere in this book, but suffice to say it is the sort of dialogue so boring it causes companions to attempt to pierce their ears with chopsticks and ingest their ravioli by way of their aural canal; conversation which causes would-be lovers to suddenly stiffen and fall forward, or ask a neighbouring table if they mind one more.

Firstly there is delivery — an Abominable Conversationalist talks too loudly, too quickly and too often. Pepper your conversation with fetid phrases like:

☞ 'You remind me of an ex-boyfriend.'
☞ 'I was only reading about that in *Penthouse* the other day.'
☞ 'Is that your hair's natural colour?'

Many good Abominable Conversationalists will try to turn the conversation with their would-be lover to the subject of sex, with lines like: 'I left my last girlfriend because she couldn't keep up with me.'

This can be followed up with a public administering of eye-drops and an explanation that you were 'up all night!'

An alternate tack taken by other Abominable Conversationalists is staring knowingly into their partner's eyes for many minutes without speaking. Finally you say something which bears no relationship to the previous conversation, but which you have deduced from the look in your partner's eyes: 'Don't you wish we could live in a world where we wouldn't have to wear clothes, where there was no disease, where people made love everywhere, all the time . . .'

The preferred method used by third-stage Abominable Conversationalists to drive their partners into abject boredom is a gross assumption about the future of their relationship, which at this point exists only on the strength of a half-eaten pasta dish. You spice your conversation with comments like:
☞ 'When I bring the boss and his wife around to our place for dinner . . .'
☞ 'We'll pack the kids off somewhere . . .'
☞ 'When we're old in a nursing home together . . .'
and:
☞ 'I plan to be making love to you when I'm eighty!'

The Sorrow of Sex

At some point even the most rejected failures face the reality of sex.
Usually they faint.
But occasionally they remain conscious, and this is what they do (assuming their partner is human):

Case Study

THE SCENE

The two lovers have entered his abode after many bottles of wine at that new little Italian place. As she seats herself on his couch he busies himself spraying Glen 20 around yesterday's washing up. He pours her an 'Orgasm' cocktail and plays a little Barry Manilow (a couple of tracks from Barry's Ethiopian famine relief concert . . . the one he recorded in New York because the strong feeling in Ethiopia was that they weren't *that* hungry). She swoons to Barry, or is it the unwashed sofa? He attempts to kiss her. His slobbering drenches her collar and for a moment she revives.

Then the moment is lost, as she kisses him back.

FAILED FOREPLAY (THE ART OF NON-AROUSAL)

His tongue is like a circus performer — he cracks it like a whip, flings it about, taming the wild lion of her soul. At the end of this her mouth feels as though it has gone eighteen rounds with an out of control electric toothbrush. If not actually aroused she is comfortably numb from the lips down, and thus ready to continue.

He undresses her rhythmically to Barry Manilow; she purrs and inhales the air redolent with Glen 20. Having brought her to nakedness he then removes his clothes.

Meticulously.

He sensually strips his socks from his feet, folding them and placing them next to his carefully folded shirt and trousers.

As he lies romantically next to her on the couch, so much of his attention is taken up with trying not to roll off the couch that it is some minutes before he realises the fingers sensually roaming his body are his own. He corrects the mistake quickly before she notices and winds up his pre-coital conversation skills:

'I wonder what they'd say at work if they could see us now ' he whispers,
'I want you as much as you want me . . .'
and finally:
'Wow . . .'

COITUS MAXIMUS:

With some masters of carnal disappointment the term 'sleeping with' becomes literal. But most are would-be sex gods who perform with the illusion that there is a row of judges lining the bedroom wall with little cards in their hands.

With Barry Manilow providing the rhythm, the Dionysian One leaps about the bed, into position after position without losing a beat; he is a blur of sexual frenzy. The fact that the subject of his lust feels much like a bean chair in a tumble drier has no bearing on the matter, as the judges begin scribbling on their little cards. In an effort to sway the undecided, the Bedroom Bacchus propels himself and his bean chair from the bed and dances around the room, holding her aloft and howling as he makes her almost complete as a woman. Within sight of a perfect ten he dives back onto the bed for his climax, clinching the gold medal with the recitation of a variety of phrases:

'Do it! Do it!'
'Yes, yes!'
'No, no!'
'Do it for me babe!'
'Do it! Yes, Yes!'
and:
'It's me! It's me!'

This last utterance often shocks the sex god's love slave back into the hideous reality of the moment, but it is too late and he mistakes her screams for ecstasy as he sees the judge's score.

'Yes, Yes!'

Post-coital Depression:

With the confidence that can only come from knowing, surely and securely, that one is the best in the world at a particular act (and dreaming blissfully of what his completed woman will tell the other girls at work), the Lovin' Legend shifts gear with his post-coital commentary. He has, after all, thrilled her like no other, taken her inhibitions and conquered them with his awesome sexual ability! Whatever he says she will worship him in the hope than some day he might bring her back to his Palace of Pleasure!

'GEEEZ!'
he murmurs sensually.

But she is asleep, no doubt replaying their intimacy in her dreams, which will also no doubt mean that she will awake wanting more. He will have to oblige, he supposes, as he too drifts off to sleep and dreams populated by gladiators . . .

'Oh God!!!' she screams before rushing to the shower. The only other words she utters before fleeing the Palace of Pleasure are also when she is in the shower:

'Do you have any Ajax?'

How to Have the
Unhappiest Day of Your Life

Chapter 7

The words 'until death us do part' are more than occasionally taken literally by this group of Fast-track Failures. Marriage is the ideal breeding ground of paranoia, self-doubt, and the other necessities for failure in the nineties.

Except for those freaks in southern American states who magnify their pain through polygamy, the marital structure is similar throughout society. But the despair levels one can reach within marriage remain unique from person to person.

If you are considering walking down the aisle and have conclusively determined your would-be spouse isn't simply asking you for help at the supermarket, then you would do well to consider the following pitfalls of the marital state, so you can spot them coming and position yourself to drop neatly in.

Now marriage must necessarily and unfortunately involve a wedding. It's a hassle but it's the law! And it is at the wedding that all the trouble begins . . .

We're Only Having a Small Ceremony

WRONG!

The average marriage party includes relatives for whom the word 'distant' was invented. It is in the planning for the wedding that you, the soon-to-be-blissful couple, realise your respective family trees are in fact part of a genetic Black Forest. From a catering job for thirty guests, which the bride's father assures everyone could be accomplished with a barbecue and a few casks of moselle, the reception becomes a feeding program large enough to qualify it as a registered charity. Kith and kin, who you thought existed only in your childhood nightmares, turn up and act so familiarly it plants the deep suspicion in you that these inbreds may have been hiding in the house all these years.

Not only does the reception balloon to beyond the population of many former Soviet states, but the accoutrements increase as well. No longer is the station wagon a fit form of transport for you: it has to be a fleet of identically tinted limousines, the combined hourly rate of which is more than sufficient to buy a small Japanese car.

The dress is so expensive it seems to have involved a customised breeding program for a better variety of silkworm and the personal attention of Pierre Cardin.

And the outpouring of dollars is not limited to immediate family members of a soon-to-be-ecstatic couple.

The wedding register is more like a cash register, as the most expensive store in town must be chosen at which to post a list of gifts you *expect* to receive. Some guests look at the gift list and laugh. But others will bankrupt themselves on a designer waffle-maker or combination coffee brewer/alarm clock, or a microwave toaster, or any one of the utterly useless appliances which you know you will need to make marriage that little bit more perfect.

The final aim of a soon-to-be-conjugal couple is to have every last detail of the wedding 'just right'. For example, if perfection in the invitation cards is not achieved, the standard response is a tribal wailing and gnashing of teeth. If the caterers can't do salmon, or only have the 'other' brand of pink champagne, both sets of in-laws and their children must gather and weep uncontrollably. The modern protocol of marriage also involves ritual telephone calls — at least twenty per day by each member of the family to each other member of the family to 'check on things'.

It is in the pre-wedding stage that a soon-to-be-connubial couple, looking to your future together, cast off your last links with the past.

Your friends.

You achieve this by raising the subject of your up-coming marriage on the half hour; from a breathless blow by blow description of the decision-making process involved in choosing chips or mashed potato for the main course, to a loud public cogitation on the topic of disbelief, as evidenced by the following oft-repeated phrases:

☞ 'I don't believe this is going to happen.'
☞ 'I don't believe this is happening to me.'
☞ 'I don't believe this is going to happen to me so soon.'
☞ 'I never believed I would get married.'
☞ 'Me? Can you believe it?'
☞ 'I can't believe I will be married in a week.'

and:

☞ 'I can't believe we're having raspberry ripple ice-cream for dessert!'

THE BIG DAY

Once the dialectic of disbelief has been completed, you, the soon-to-be-getting-undressed-couple, find yourselves at the business end of a church you have never been in before. Now, at this point you both usually become extremely nervous that you will forget your lines — it is all part of the Western tradition of marriage.

Hundreds of man-hours and thousands of dollars have brought

you to this point and now you're on your own. If you fail to remember your lines, if you stumble or faint on the way into or out of the church, you will be marked as irretrievable failures by both families for the rest of your lives. If you forget to kiss each other, try to kiss through a veil, try to kiss the bridesmaid, or forget your names when signing the marriage certificate, then the game is over — you will be spurned even by the near-zygote brother who has been roped in to be a flower boy. Yes, if you fall over during the bridal waltz, forget the name of a relative you have not seen since before you were conceived, or jam your feet in the limo door and fall out, you are history.

RIP — the couple who couldn't even get married properly!

This is possibly as close to Nirvana as an aspiring failure ever gets.

However, the regrettable reality is that your wedding is the only time in your life when you can be a complete idiot and people will forgive you.

A soon-to-be-bouncy-bouncy-couple can do no wrong and waltz into the reception fresh from the wedding of the century.

'I wish there'd been some royalty here,'

whispers one remote relation to another.

'We could've shown 'em a thing or two!'

The reception itself is a coming together of all the various strands of mind-numbing conversation known to humanity, culminating in eye-glazing impromptu speeches by people the marital couple can only hope have turned up for the wrong wedding. (The thought that *your* family could throw up such obvious examples of pre-vertical man is too depressing to contemplate — after all, you *do* plan to have children.)

At a certain point the thought of state-sanctioned sex becomes far more attractive to a soon-to-be-intimate-couple than the prospect of hearing one more story about how embarrassing you were as children . . .

Look At Us — We're Sleeping Together!

Honeymooner Hell begins with a happy couple making the mistake of *mentioning* to others that you are on your honeymoon. Fellow holidayers then suspect that — as opposed to them — you are **actually doing it** and not just thinking about doing it! Thereafter, all the other residents of the small South Pacific atoll which rose from the sea in a volcanic eruption of bad taste (complete with heart-shaped swimming pool and perennial buffet service) stare at you and titter things to each other like:

☞ 'I wonder how many times they did it last night?'

☞ 'Do you think she looks disappointed this morning, Fred?'

and:

☞ 'Why's he limping, Muriel?'

You are ostentatiously offered oysters by the atoll's self-appointed wit. The new husband is told: 'Don't drink too much, son — got to perform, remember.' The new wife benefits from those much older and wiser than her: 'Keep him hungry, lovie.'

In the end it is as though the entire population of a small South Pacific atoll are participants in one hideously huge, arcane, polygamous honeymoon ceremony, fuelled by drinks which resemble toxic waste dumps, a buffet service which looks like a public tip in a fishing town and at which two people expend all the sexual energy for the general enjoyment of everyone else!

Settling Down — Having a Renovator's Nightmare

To assure long-term misery and despondency for its occupants, the marital dwelling must be chosen with care. Most importantly, *it must need renovation*!

'It will be fun darling, we can spend weekends painting!'

is usually the first innocent step towards turning the family home not only into an utter disaster area, but into a 24-hour bank for a variety of tradesmen; for the common or garden variety Happy Couple neglect to face up to the fact that the painting ends up being the *last* act in the process of renovation (the one that occurs so the house will fetch a good price for the divorce settlement) . . .

THE STEPS TO RENOVATION CATASTROPHE

You are told by the painter, before painting can happen the walls need to be re-plastered.

Yes, advises the plasterer solemnly, but before the walls can be replastered they have to be re-built.

No problem, counsels the builder, but these walls shouldn't have been built in the first place, so the house will have to be re-designed.

A snack, murmurs the architect, taking up expensive time to sigh, but your block is damp and sloping, and will have to be examined by a geologist.

Hmmm, snorts the geologist, there's a substratum of clay and likely as not when the Pacific plate hits the coast, the house will simply fall into the sea.

We can fix it, says the engineer whose work includes the Snowy Mountains Scheme and Operation 'Desert Storm', but it will be expensive . . .

Now the block is stable, confirms the architect with a longer and more expensive sigh, we can re-design the house but it will be expensive.

We can build that, promises the builder, it will be expensive but we *should* be finished in a month, barring any 'unforeseen events'.

At this point, with the painter and plasterer still distant specks on the horizon (where they have been joined by an electrician, a plumber, a carpet-layer, a fireplace installer, the central air-conditioning man, a bloke from the gas company and a crowd of others) you, the Happy Couple, are sitting in what you once hoped would be your lounge room reading a dictionary aloud to each other:

'"**Unforeseen**",' says the husband. 'Not to see beforehand or have prescience of . . . unable to make provision for. From the Latin "*unforseenum*" meaning "big time screw-up".'

'"**Event**",' reads the wife. 'An occurrence of some importance, esp. when used with "unforeseen". From the Greek "*eventus*" meaning "it will happen, except in the case of temple builders".'

But apart from the woes visited upon the married couple externally, what are they like internally? What kind of spouses are they? Are they failures?

We all know the traditional Mr and Mrs No-hoper — the beer-swilling husband and the fault-finding wife — but this is the nineties! Whole new sub-species of marital non-achievers have evolved since those earlier dinosaurs.

How to Become a Hopeless Husband

For ease of reference, the major inspirational types have been summarised in the following categories:

HOPELESS HUSBAND TYPE 1: MR MALADROIT

Mr Maladroit is the sort of man utterly unsuited to cohabitation, period. His primary failing is in the area of basic motor functions like bed making, dish washing, and floor sweeping (though he also has trouble on the toilet). Mr Maladroit has apparently never learnt, or is incapable of learning, most of those things which distinguish man from beast: cooking food, washing himself, wearing clothes properly.

Mr Maladroit does have one highly developed, uniquely human talent.

Self-justification.

A few sample excuses:

- ☞ 'Why make the bed when I'm only going to lie on it again in twelve hours?'
- ☞ 'The clothes are only going to get dirty again whether I wash them or not!'
- ☞ 'That's why I always use paper plates!'
- ☞ 'There's a limit to how much dirt can collect on the floor, so if you leave it alone for a while it will stabilise.'

For the ill-fated woman who finds herself legally attached to Mr Maladroit, there are only two choices: put up with it, or train him. Most women opt for the latter, using a reward/ punishment system whereby every motor function successfully managed by Mr Maladroit entitles him to continued feeding, and every failure to perform is punishable by anything from restricted sexual access through to forcing him to eat his ice-cream with chopsticks.

HOPELESS HUSBAND TYPE 2: THE MALE FEMINIST

A Male Feminist is a husband who turns household chores into an ideology. Every task is loaded with gender politics and must be examined carefully to determine which spouse should complete the job.

The typical dilemma faced by the Male Feminist is in the area of cooking — the Male Feminist's immediate instinct is to do all the cooking and thus make up for the decades of macho expectation that there would actually be a meal on the table every night! However, after intense discussion with his partner and the consultation of a few standard texts on the subject, the Male Feminist begins to convince himself that providing his partner with food is giving in to some antediluvian providing instinct of 'man the hunter', which is where the whole problem of sexism and gender-baiting began in the first place.

Can he really take the risk that he may be the catalyst for starting the cycle of oppression all over again?

Finally, with great ideological firmness, he advises his partner that he will fulfil the passive-subservient role of waiting for the meal and trusts she is overjoyed at his gender awareness.

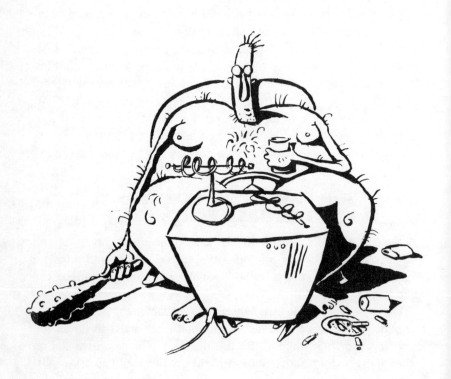

HOPELESS HUSBAND TYPE 3:
THE HAIRY MAN

This type of husband is a particularly nineties' individual, always on the lookout for aspects of his marriage which might be eroding his masculinity.

The belief of the Hairy Man is that true manhood has been whittled away over the years by giving ground to women and the time has come to strike back! Luckily for wives of Hairy Men, they do not actually have to put up with him all that much, as he normally spends long periods of time gallivanting in the bush with other Hairy Men, chanting feel-good man words like:

'Man! Man! Man!'

and:

'Men! Men! Men!'

and then:

'Man! Man! Man!'

again.

But when they are at home, Hairy Men will attempt to understand their wives' uniquely feminine expression of concern about facets of their primal relationship . . . like 'who cooks dinner?'

Unfortunately, although the Hirsute One will 'work through' the woman-worry faced by his wife, the end result is that no self-respecting Hairy Man will sacrifice his cajones for the sake of appeasing female frailty, and after retiring to the toilet for a few cleansing rounds of 'Man! Man! Man!', the warrior king returns to his tribal gathering room for roast haunch of beast and a mug of ale!

How to Become a
Woeful Wife

In this equal-opportunity world there are female equivalents of all the above Hopeless Husband types, however, we will briefly outline a few female-specific sub-species of Sub-standard Spouse.

WOEFUL WIFE TYPE 1:
THE POWERSPOUSE

To the Powerspouse, marriage is a merger between two highly independent individuals who believe their market effectiveness is increased by a pooling of talents.

ERGO — the Powerspouse approaches every household act with the same dynamic vigour as every workplace act. A dinner party is not just a dinner party; there is a greater reason for it than the pallid excuse of 'having fun'! No — the aim of a good dinner party strategy is to bring together wildly different people for a think-tank at which food just happens to be served. Hence the Powerhome becomes the venue for meetings between kindergarten teachers, bikers, corner store owners and flute players.

WOEFUL WIFE TYPE 2:
THE WILDWOMAN

The main distinguishing feature which separates Wildwomen from other wives is a deep and abiding interest in interior designing. The 'wild' in her title stems from the Wildwoman's attitude towards colour, cloth and, particularly, cost, in her quest for interior design perfection.

Wildwomen typically throw parties to celebrate the wallpaper having been successfully hung, or the spiral staircase installed, or the arrival of the appliances.

The food served at these vogue festivals is normally small cracker biscuits and peanut butter, as the family coffers have been emptied by the reason for the party.

But they are happy affairs, bringing together disparate members of the community who probably had not seen each other since the carpets were laid!

WOEFUL WIFE TYPE 3:
THE AMBIGUOUSPOUSE

The Ambiguouspouse can be recognised by the following conversational style:

> **Ambiguouspouse:** 'Which do you think looks better on me dear, the red dress or the green dress?'
>
> **Husband:** 'The green dress, dear.'
>
> **Ambiguouspouse:** '*What's* wrong with the red dress!'

The Ambiguouspouse believes marriage is one great guessing game where she asks the questions, her husband answers, and then she decides whether or not he is correct.

> **Ambiguouspouse:** 'Do you think lamb or beef for the dinner party?'
>
> **Husband:** 'Beef . . .'
>
> **Ambiguouspouse:** 'I thought you *liked* lamb!'
>
> **Husband:** 'I love that perfume, dear.'
>
> **Ambiguouspouse (suspiciously):** 'You've *never* noticed it before.'
>
> **Husband:** 'I bought some flowers for you, dear.'
>
> **Ambiguouspouse:** '*Why?*'

It is a system guaranteed to keep most husbands well and truly under control. In the end, a strategic querulous 'uh huh' from the Ambiguouspouse will bring most men to their knees, babbling apologetically and begging for forgiveness.

Having achieved complete alienation within your marriage, you can now move on to the next step of Fast-track Failure in the family.

Breeding!

How to Raise Psychotic Children

Chapter 8

*O*ne of the first great shocks of childhood is realising who your parents are. The second great shock is realising it is an irrevocable situation. Fast-tracking Filial Failure through a combination of pathetic parenting and simply being a negative role model comes naturally to most. But what is not so commonly known is how to harness your children to contribute to your own mental breakdown.

The first decision one has to make in raising psychotic children is the decision to actually have them. (A strong case could be put, for example, that some readers of this book should be actively prevented from breeding. For others, attempted conception should be made a criminal offence!)

Attempted conception can often be the beginning and end of failure in this life area, because of low sperm count, wrong position, you have a headache, or you find your spouse sexually repulsive.

An interesting aid to '**conception — worst case scenario**' can be explored through the application of sexual hints found in many self-help pregnancy books. Most of these involve sexual positions which attempt to endow the sperm with additional momentum to assure it travels all the way up the fallopian highway. These jet-propelled sperm are most often ejaculated after what would appear, to an outside observer, to be a complex dance manoeuvre, followed by a hop, skip and jump, a swan dive in the pike position with a twist onto the bed, and a final, mutual, vigorous assault by both sets of genitalia. Then **KERPOW!!!** — wimp sperm, which was moments before using water-wings, is now rocketing upwards irresistibly.

Unfortunately, after one of these attacks the target egg often looks like a wooden duck after a long day in a shooting gallery, and the bedroom gymnasts responsible are usually sidelined for weeks with tendon and bone damage. The outside observer is normally spotted pretty swiftly by a neighbour, arrested as a pervert, and taken off to gaol.

However, let us assume that through a combination of luck and enthusiasm, the state of conception is reached by you, our generic couple. There, floating blissfully in your gene pool, is the child you have been dreaming of.

Now what? you think. Wait out the nine months? Not on your nelly! Have the child born with a disadvantage?

There is much to be done during the critical time of pregnancy to nurture your own neuroses and probably create a few in the kid as well! It is one of the most important stages in raising psychotic children.

The Prego-phone Stage

The actual gadget you — as-parents-who-would-be-perfect — plan to use to intrude on the only nine months of peace your child will ever get, looks at first glance as though it belongs in the plumbing supplies section of a hardware store. One end of the Prego-phone is a mouthpiece, the other is a sucker — between is a length of tube. The mother-who-would-be-ideal licks the sucker and attaches it to her stomach . . . and now, through the mouthpiece, the development of the child-who-would-be-opera-star, academic, poet, novelist, tycoon, talk-back radio host etc, really begins!

Central to the Prego-phone Stage is the conviction that communication with the womb is possible **(it helps if you also have a healthy belief in the continued existence of Elvis).**

Anything can be piped through the mouthpiece to the soon-to-be-born-genius. You can try a variety of sounds — conversation, classical music, poetry (your own), television (the ABC of course!), and an intelligent form of talk-back radio. **(Also central to the Prego-phone Stage is the belief that an intelligent form of talk-back radio exists.)** It is crucial to act with the assumption that your child actually *wants* to listen to the swill being piped down to it. To assume otherwise is to imagine being trapped in an elevator for nine months, trying to sleep through the lift muzak!

You then decide to take it in turns to converse with your child through the Prego-phone during the nine months, knowing, as parents-who-would-be-faultless, you each have something to say as separate but complementary individuals. You talk about the little things that make up your lives . . . what went wrong at work, life inside a supermarket, the interesting frame on your Renoir print.

And, most often, descriptions of the life awaiting your child at home:

☞ 'I'm washing up now, honey. When you're born you can help your mother and me wash up — won't that be fun? Washing up as a family!'

☞ 'Your father and I love this movie, especially this part. I'll let you hear it . . . there! The bit where Clark Gable says "I love you". I'll rewind it for you. Honey — could you rewind the video? There!'

☞ 'I'm dusting now honeybunchkins. When you're born you can help your mother and me dust — won't that be fun? Dusting as a family!'

And so it comes to pass that after nine months trapped in an elevator listening to mind-numbing anecdotes which couldn't wait until old age, the lift doors finally open on the ground floor of life and the child prepares to enter this world about which it has already heard so much — and about which it is having serious second thoughts. **Still, it reasons, anything is better than this! They might even have earplugs out there!**

But what's this — a waterslide?

Lamaze, Le Chic

The birthing method is the next major decision to be made by parents-who-would-be-wonderful. The pregnancy books you have bought argue seriously for a 'peaceful' transition from womb to world. Most often this involves preparing a small plastic pool full of tepid water, herbs, exotic salts and, occasionally, jelly.

In the normal course of events, the small plastic pool sits in the centre of the lounge room and leaks slowly on to the carpet, as the mother-who-would-be-tranquil is rushed to hospital for a caesarean with an epidural drip!

But occasionally the child actually cooperates with these alternate birthing methods and doesn't get stuck on the way out. What faces it upon arrival into the world seems much like the inside of the elevator from whence it has come — subdued lighting, reddish tones, and those same voices it has heard for the last nine months chanting 'Om, Om, Om'.

That is, of course, before the flashbulbs pop.

Cecil B. De Maternity Ward!

Of course, the birth must be recorded!

After all, as a couple-who-would-be-in-Florence-at-Christmas, you assure each other: 'We *will* stop at one!'

In the final stage of pregnancy (the stage when one or both parents run out of things to blurt into the Prego-phone), the father-who-would-be-at-Cannes becomes a purchasing blur in photographic and recording equipment stores.

The result is that shortly after the lift doors slide open, the child is faced with a paparazzi bedlam of flashbulbs and lights. There are at least two cameras (in case one fails or the processing destroys the film), a video camera for the moving pictures, a cassette player to record the whole event — and over it all a commentary!

'Push, yes push!'
or:
'OM! OM! OM!'

Hurry — Another Ten Minutes and it'll be a <u>Virgo</u>!

It is perhaps the most significant question to be determined when planning a family. It is something to which notice has to be given long before conception; a determinant you, as parents-who-would-cover-all-bases, have agonised over. And now, as the moment of birth draws inexorably closer, what will be the result of your dice toss?

What will the child's star sign be?

Yes — it is not only male genitalia that has to be on the ascendant for the perfect conception, it has to be Uranus!

For the child's position in the zodiac is fundamental to how he or she will succeed and in what:

'There is success and success!' you, as parents-who-would-be-prudent, mutter, sitting in bed with your calendar:

'We know what a *successful* Scorpio is all about!'

The astrological decision is made even more difficult if:

(a) It is the second child and thus must complement the first in the zodiac while still retaining as many chances to make it as a Virgo can have.

(b) The parents read too many popular magazines.

Negative Nomenclature

Choosing a name for your child is crucial in determining whether it gets off on the wrong foot or not. Americans have a special knack at picking utterly ludicrous names for their children (eg Flip Spiceland, Skip Guntrash, Storm Field, Moon Unit Zappa), but Australians are fairly adept at this form of applied misery too. Some parents are so bereft of original thought they simply tack their surname on again, resulting in children called Smithy Smith, Sharon Sharen, Lip Lipman, Mary Maryland. (This technique of Negative Nomenclature has the added benefit that the child is almost guaranteed to develop a stutter through the simple act of pronouncing its name.)

The other factor many parents seem to take on board is ensuring their child's name can be easily abridged into an obscenity (eg Leititia — which in the nefarious nicknaming of the schoolyard will invariably become 'Titty').

But you may want none of this naming inanity! You, as parents-who-would-be-unique, may want to choose the most original name ever chosen! Annthraski or Marionioque? Gardenella, Gwertz-tramina or Soulezpunzelle?

Perhaps that name which means 'Fighter with Steel' in a neanderthal dialect; or 'Rose floating on ocean with dewdrops' in ancient Hindi[1].

1. The author has never understood the latter method of naming children. These languages wouldn't have died out if they were so interesting! Perhaps these types of names are chosen by parents in the hope that one day their child will be walking down the street and meet a person fluent in ancient Hindi who will say:

'Ah — "Rose floating on the ocean with dewdrops"! You must surely have educated parents. Let me give you a fabulous job and this very expensive present for them!'

Decisions, Decisions!

The all-wood, chemical-free bedroom furniture, the Italian designed pram, the 'Dom Perignon' baby formula, the disposable nappy made out of recycled tyres which must nevertheless change colour at the slightest hint of excreta, the ideologically sound jigsaws and socially relevant books — decisions, decisions!

At what age should the third language be taught — six or nine months? Japanese or German? Violin or piano? Classical or jazz? Decisions, decisions!

Do I let my child see me naked or not? To smack or not to smack? Work through problems with child or scream and shout? Trust babysitter or not? Is babysitter a child molester or not? Assuming all babysitters are child molesters, is this one violent or not?

Decisions, decisions!

Becoming a Negative Role Model

Once one has had and named one's child, and purchased the plethora of paranoia-preventing-parental-props, one can move on to the easy part.

Becoming a negative role model.

For most parents this involves doing nothing out of the ordinary — but perhaps these hints might help those of you in danger of becoming a positive influence on your offspring.

HOW TO BECOME A PASSIVE–NEGATIVE ROLE MODEL

A good example of this type is the father who simply doesn't think. So, wanting to get an early night on Christmas Eve and simultaneously assist his four-year-old son's ascent to manhood, the Failure Father suggests that *this* year the boy can dress up as Santa and distribute the presents.

Or the Failure Father will do the St Nick bit, then fall asleep forgetting to take his suit off, so come Christmas Day his children find their mother in bed with Santa.

You can take your children to see movies like *Gremlins* and *Teenage Mutant Ninja Turtles* and neglect to tell them that they are not documentaries.

Or you can engage in the simplest kind of parental lethargy — like leaving a personal cheque in the tooth fairy glass.

HOW TO BECOME A 'LIFE'S-A-HARD-LESSON' ROLE MODEL

You are determined that *your* child will have *all* the clues! You ask your children's advice in business and take the relevant sum out of their pocket money if the deal turns sour. You teach your children the ins and outs of school politics; how to form alliances to crush the little guy; how to snivel to the school bully; grossly sycophantic things they can do in class; and how to cheat.

For parents for whom Life was a hard lesson simply because you are as stupid as pig dogs, books with titles like *Fun with Crossbows*, *Pyrotechnics for Pleasure and Profit*, and *Great Bank Robbers* are often appropriate gifts for your children. You are also often found being thrown out of kindergarten plays for screaming 'More!!! More!!!' incessantly after your child's walk-on role.

HOW TO BECOME A
MEGA-ENLIGHTENED ROLE MODEL

You are utterly liberal with your children. If the little individuals feel like smearing their nappies on the saucepans you tell yourself it is just an expression of their uniqueness. If your child wants to swallow the goldfish, you say it's embryonic performance art (and it's not as though goldfish are an endangered species!).

Finally, you buy your child Kafka picture books, and put camembert and water crackers in their kindy lunchbox.

But remember — there is no need to put yourself through everything described in this chapter in order to fail as a parent. The alternative to all of the above is to nurture your children, give them every chance in Life, and then when they inevitably succeed . . .

Envy them!

Dismal Divorce

Chapter 9

Perhaps the greatest advice you can take in the field of divorce is this. Why take the step of marriage? Just find someone you hate and buy them a house! To illustrate this, and set our course for truly dismal divorce, let us look inside the mind of a recent divorcee.

CASE STUDY

He calls 'A Current Affair' constantly, asking them to do a story on the injustice committed to him. His old friends have all found other friends; he hates his new friends, who are all recently divorced. He hates people with the same first name as his ex-wife. He hates people with the same initials as his ex-wife. He hates people the same age, height, eye colour, hair colour, build, and people who live in the same suburb . . . as his ex-wife!

He is divorced.

His spouse got the gold mine and he got the shaft. Someone he once loved he now wants to have kneecapped. He sends his ex-wife encouraging letters purporting to come from the Albanian embassy offering hassle-free immigration. But how did he achieve this utter misery from what had seemed to be an amicable parting of the ways between two rational adults?

He took the first fateful step towards divorce-caused-despondency and depression. He hired a lawyer. Then he took the second fateful step. He believed his lawyer.

And she believed hers.

The above is an insight into the mind of just one of the many types of Fast-track Failures who choose divorce as their route to ruin. The individual described above belongs to the major grouping in this field. He is a believer in the post-marital technique known by its technical title of . . .

Revenge At All Costs!:
Dismal Divorcee Type 1

The revenge-driven spouse is the kind who keeps private detective agencies in business, and conversations like this happening in a million gumshoes' offices around the world:

'Sir, the photograph is grainy, we can't actually tell whether that shape is a lover or a shopping bag.'

'That's it! Bitch — I've got you now! Hah! hah! hah!'

Revengaholics are obsessed with proving their spouse's infidelity, their inadequacy as a parent, their ability as a tax cheat, and (where alimony is concerned) their good health and excellent employment opportunities.

The first step most Revengaholics must take is learning how to lie convincingly to themselves: she was promiscuous . . . he was a drunk . . . she beat the kids . . . he beat the kids . . . she starved him . . . he psychologically abused her . . . he drilled her teeth as she slept . . . she tried to administer enemas on him as he watched the football. Most Revengaholics just make it up. They get a few ideas from popular literature and television, but mostly it is their own work.

The most important technique in becoming a successful Revengaholic is to *listen carefully to your lawyer!*

Often lawyers are bound by restrictive regulations on ethics set up to help people like the Revengaholic's spouse, so much of the evidence-gathering is done by innuendo. For example, the following is an actual conversation recorded by a highly paid private detective between a Revengaholic and his lawyer:

> Lawyer: 'Did your wife actively cause you difficulties during the course of your marriage?'
>
> Revengaholic: 'Difficulties! *You* try explaining to *your* children why your wife sticks magazine advertisements for men's jeans on the bedroom ceiling!'
>
> Lawyer: 'Is it fair to say your relationship generated a great deal of stress for you and your wife?'
>
> Revengaholic: 'I told you — don't ever use that word!!!'
>
> Lawyer: 'Stress?'
>
> Revengaholic: 'Wife!!!!'
>
> Lawyer: 'But there *was* stress in the marriage?'
>
> Revengaholic: 'Only if you call stress being kept awake night after night because your wife keeps a tape-recorder on in the hope of catching you talking in your sleep!'

The rule of thumb for a Revengaholic is that anything your lawyer suggests, you can exaggerate.

If the divorce decision goes against you in court, you stop at nothing. The most common route is calling television programs and making outrageous claims that your spouse is involved in the white slave market; or calling the tax department and telling their inspector to look in the little drawer on the left of the bed and they'll find something very interesting; or masquerading as the police and calling a restaurant your spouse is dining at with a description of a serial killer which just happens to match your spouse's.

Or you can be more inventive — shadow your spouse, and have him or her paged in public places:

☞ 'Mr Derek Smith, your parole officer is waiting at the information booth.'

☞ 'Mrs Marla Smith, *Penthouse* magazine is waiting for you in room 1409.'

But after a while, Revengaholics either wear themselves out or spontaneously self-immolate — though as failure goes it ain't bad while it lasts!

I Understand:
Dismal Divorcee Type 2

The Understanding Ex-spouse is the kind who believes that two sane adults shouldn't let a little thing like divorce stand in the way of their being friends. You begin by giving your spouse everything:

'No take it — you deserve it!'

Then stay in touch with your ex-spouse, making frequent phone calls, buying drinks, sending out invitations to dinner. In conversations with your previous partner, an Understanding Ex-spouse tells little stories from the marriage, reminiscences which show how little the whole thing affected you.

When your ex-spouse gets a new partner, an Understanding One invites them both out for drinks, and over for dinner, ensuring you pepper your conversation with *bon mots* about *your* marriage, comparing it to *their* current relationship:

☞ 'Of course we always liked scrambled eggs for breakfast; I'd cook and she'd do coffee. Do you do that?'

☞ 'We would always do it in front of the TV — where do you do it now?'

An Understanding Ex-spouse ends up minding your ex's new children while the new happy couple go on holidays.

One can always recognise an Understanding Ex-spouse in the tertiary stage by his miserable answering machine message:

'You have reached what used to be the number for Marla and Derek Smith, but now only Derek lives here — Marla has married Frank and has two new children, Skip and Gipper . . . Please leave your message after the sigh.'

The Divorce Obsessive:
Dismal Divorcee Type 3

The Divorce Obsessive is the type who believes it is not only right that one lose one's spouse, children and most earthly possessions in a divorce, but that one should lose all one's friends in the process.

A Divorce Obsession begins during the divorce proceeding. You swear mutual friends of you and your ex-spouse to utter confidence and then use any dirt they tell you on the witness stand the following day.

You invite your friends to your divorce proceedings, or around for drinks at your place after each day's court appearance to view video tapes of the testimony. After the court decision, you continually talk about your divorce at dinner parties.

You then go through the detached, cynical stage and can be heard at parties saying: 'Oh yes, this isn't the end for me. One day I plan to meet a new girl, settle down, have a couple of kids and then in a few years divorce her.'

The first question you ask any new person you meet is: 'Are you divorced?'

At weddings you make a point of telling divorce jokes and quote divorce statistics to the newlyweds. As their car speeds off down honeymoon boulevard you mutter loudly:

'They'll be back!'

Recovery and Rebuilding

All you have read above is negative, counterproductive action, invaluable to any determined Dismal Divorcee. However, at some point in your irretrievable marital breakdown and subsequent divorce you must begin to rebuild your life in order to explore other areas of failure.

There are many ways of getting over the trauma of divorce, but perhaps the most effective is aversion therapy. Below is a step-by-step guide to using this form of treatment at home:

Step-By-Step Guide to Divorce Recovery

Step 1. Look through the old family photo albums, and whenever you see your spouse, cause yourself some bodily pain: slap yourself, poke your hand with a fork, or bite your tongue.

Step 2. After a week or two of this you will have a pathologically advanced aversion to your ex-spouse and a strong desire never to see him or her again.

(Unfortunately you will also have an advanced aversion to using forks.)

Step 3. You have now done in two weeks what the legal system could have done for you in two days, but dammit!

You've done it yourself!

Part IV
FAILURE AT A PROFESSIONAL LEVEL

Seeking Professional Help

(Or, Failing That, Going to a Psychiatrist)

Chapter 10

At one stage or another we all feel let down by our miserable existence and get the urge to reciprocate, to strike back at Life. Unless these moments of angst occur on high floors near open windows or while jogging beside a freeway, the simple remedy for them is a quick lie down.

However, a significant proportion of the population has developed the knack of turning these occasional moments of depression into a full-blown Formula for Failure.

They are called Imitation or Ersatz Loons.

Ersatz Loons are people who experience passing melancholic episodes and convince themselves that they are symptoms of something else, something more serious and, most importantly, something covered by health insurance.

They believe they need therapy.

They believe they're cracking up!

Ersatz Loons come to revel in their imminent insanity, their burgeoning neuroses and pending psychoses. Why? Because it is one of the most accessible areas of personal deterioration there is, and one can actually *pay* someone else to do all the hard work.

A psychiatrist — for those not familiar with the term — is a highly trained individual hired to convince those who want convincing (ie the Ersatz Loon) that they are indeed cracked, potty, not-all-there or simply a sandwich short of a picnic; in short — that they are gilt-edged, certifiable loopies!

Come for a trip into this fascinating field of failure. Come and spend quality time with three Ersatz Loons, enter their peculiar worlds and learn how you too can become persuaded of your own mental shortcomings.

Note: **The following case studies are all male, as we all know sex has nothing to do with psychology.**

Ersatz Loon Type 1
(The Therapaddict)

Externally the Therapaddict looks just like you or me (ie either hideously ugly or extraordinarily attractive). It is his internal mechanisms which mark the Therapaddict as a passenger on one of the faulty dodgem cars in the great festival of Life.

The Therapaddict is on a constant search for himself, and is four years into an analysis which he hopes will finally provide the proof that **HE REALLY DOES HAVE A PROBLEM!**

The alternative reason our Therapaddict is in analysis is because he learnt long ago that shelling over large quantities of money seemed to be his only way of finding someone who would listen to him talk. But regardless of his motivation, we now join him to study the psychopathology of his everyday life.

He is at breakfast. He is staring intently at the patterns made on his plate by a dribbling boiled egg, trying to gain an insight into his unconscious through the shape of the yolk blots. Satisfied by the morning's ritual Rorschach Test that he is a deeply troubled individual and has woken up with his problem intact, the Therapaddict scoffs his egg and decides to try a little free association with his wife.

'Morning dear!' she says.
'Tapir!' he exclaims.
'Like a coffee?' she says.
'Quince!' he replies.

Yes, no doubt about it, he thinks happily, I've still got it!

He kisses her lightly on the cheek as he prepares to leave for work, and muses just how much she reminds him of his mother.

On the bus, our Therapaddict amuses himself by giving his id free range and imagining what he would get up to with the woman in the third seat on the left. Ensuring his superego is firmly in control, he inches closer to her, and visualises himself and the target of his id becoming a blur of arms and legs, right there on the bus, in front of everyone!!!

'*Careful,*' warns his superego, '***don't you think she looks a lot like your mother?***'

Comfortably stricken by guilt feelings, and certain his Oedipal Complex is alive and well, the Therapaddict alights at his stop and begins to walk towards his office block.

As he stops at the traffic light, he gazes up at its erectness and feels a twinge of penis envy before crossing the street, glorying in his level of self-perception as he jostles through the crowd of non-loons.

He stands in the elevator as it travels upwards, and feels secure within its womb-like interior, suffering a moment of birth trauma as he gets out at his floor. He pours himself a coffee and begins slobbering as he realises how much like his mother's breast the cup looks.

Later in the day as he is compulsively stapling, the Therapaddict feels the need to find a bit more of himself and decides to free associate with his boss:

'Smith, is that report ready yet?'

'Battle of the Coral Sea.'

'Don't be an idiot, Smith!'

Whereupon the Therapaddict vents his primal scream and is promptly sent home.

Unfortunately, he has forgotten they are having a dinner party that night. He sighs sadly to himself, before realising it will be a perfect chance to match his wits with the collective unconscious. Unfortunately his understanding of the collective unconscious is only sketchy, and all he manages to achieve is to put everyone in the room to sleep. The cat is the only warm-blooded creature still awake in the household, and as the Therapaddict retires for the night it purrs thankfully.

'Snail pellets . . .' he murmurs, before falling asleep and dreaming he is flying about in a dark cave with a large horse.

But there is another kind of Fast-track Failure in the Ersatz Loon area. He is much like the Therapaddict except for one major difference. This type desperately wants to believe he is normal but **CAN'T AVOID THE OBVIOUS SIGNS!** He has, finally and under sufferance (at the urging of family members, close friends, and work colleagues), gone for 'help'. But he *knows* that once he gets into the clutches of psychiatry he is finished, washed up — a step away from seeing secret messages meant only for him printed on the labels of Vegemite jars.

He is what Freud would doubtless have called the 'Poodle Man'.

(Nothing weird about old Sigmund, huh?)

Ersatz Loon Type 2
(Poodle Man)

We find Poodle Man sitting, simpering, in a waiting room, which is tastefully decorated so as to look as little like a receiving dock for nutcases as it can.

He is quivering as he attempts to read a pre-war copy of *National Geographic* upside down. Running through his brain is the query *'How many other lunatics have fondled this?'*

Then Poodle Man remembers something his mother once said. His dear wonderful mother, his beautiful, gorgeous, slightly plump in a huggable sort of way mother . . . (**'OH GOD, IT'S HAPPENING ALREADY!'** he thinks). He remembers something his mother once said after feeding him with those slightly upturned breasts and lovely brown aureoles . . . He remembers his mother murmuring to him as she clutched him in that secret way she never used when Dad was in the room . . .

'Only people who 'ave no friends go to psych'trists!'

He thinks of his mother as he reads 'The Fate of the Vanishing Dugong' and, wondering why ancient mariners thought they were mermaids, he squints his eyes and twists the magazine in front of his face, closer and further back to see if the creature could look attractive or even like his mother . . . then he looks up.

The receptionist is staring at him fixedly.

She giggles. To Poodle Man that giggle says it all: that she's met every class of crazy and right now she is trying to classify him! Quickly he glances back to 'The Fate of the Vanishing Dugong'. She giggles again, but he knows she is just trying to catch his attention so she can stare at him fixedly again.

Right now, Poodle Man thinks, she is doodling a sketch of him and next to it writing the following words: madman, maniac, psychopath, oddball, idiot, simpleton, moron, imbecile, crackpot, crazy, loony, cretin, dimwit, fool, blockhead, dolt, dunce and buffoon, and wondering which one to tick.

As he shuffles into the psychiatrist's office, Poodle Man is sure his expression indicates that he is a brick short of a load; that the sway of his arms suggests he is not paddling with all his oars in the water; that his downcast eyes practically blare out that his elevator doesn't go to the top floor; and that the rustle of his hands in his pockets suggests his dipstick hasn't seen oil in a long time.

By now Poodle Man is *convinced* of his mental inadequacy, of his complete cerebral unworthiness. It helps him to remember, as he lies back on the couch, that the psychiatrist really doesn't want to talk to him. He is doing it for vast sums of money. He profits from wackos like him. And the more he considers how much richer the psychiatrist is becoming by the second, the more miserable Poodle Man becomes.

But it is more than just the money, he tells himself. After a few questions Poodle Man *knows* he is being used to further the psychiatrist's career, and will eventually star as a case study in a thesis called 'Impressions on a Couch'. Or perhaps his pathetic gibberings will form the cornerstone of some entirely new scientific theory! After all, if the gossip according to a few Viennese housewives was responsible for psychoanalysis, he murmurs, anything is possible . . . Certain of this, Poodle Man becomes extremely suspicious. He is careful not to mention a fondness for animals at this point. He remembers 'Little Hans'.[1]

He tells the psychiatrist patent untruths in a vain attempt to prove his normality. **NOTHING HELPS.**

At the end of a long first session on the couch, the psychiatrist speaks the fateful words to Poodle Man:

'You are the type of person who makes psychiatry such a challenging profession. I need to see you on a regular basis.'

---

1. Little Hans was an early Ersatz Loon who believed he was a bale of hay and that if he went outside his house he would promptly be eaten by a horse. Unfortunately, all of this occurred in turn-of-the-century Vienna where there was a horrifying abundance of horses on the lookout for a stray bale of hay. Luckily Sigmund Freud took pity on Hans. After years of intense psychoanalysis and a final realisation that Hans had repressed the fact that he had been covered with shredded-wheat cereal as an infant by his mother, Freud convinced the boy that horses didn't exist.

The third and final type of Ersatz Loon is one for whom Life is a complex network of avoidance. The air he breathes, the shape of today's pencil sharpeners and the noise made by low flying planes — to the Type 3 Ersatz Loon they are all part of a divinely concocted aversion therapy designed just for him.

Just about everything the Type 3 Ersatz Loon does in everyday life provokes heart palpitations, a tightness in the chest, shortness of breath and, usually, a strong desire to throw up.

He is the Phobic Fool.

Ersatz Loon Type 3
(THE PHOBIC FOOL)

The Phobic Fool is always on the lookout for something to refuse on the basis of his particular emotional or cerebral instability, a deep-seated phobia over which he has no control.

He turns down simple tasks because they involve open spaces, or enclosed spaces; suspects work colleagues of harbouring transmissible terminal diseases; and will not drive his car on the grounds that the vibrations through the steering wheel are affecting his ability to have children.

Sometime between primal and group therapy our Type 3 case study (like Ersatz Loon Type 1) came to learn one of the most important talents of being a successful crackpot — the ability to ignore the phrase:

'STOP BEING AN IDIOT.'

At work or at play, the Phobic Fool is a constant aggravation for his fellow human beings. Invite him to dinner and you also invite his phobia, which infects his every conversational contribution:

'Oh yes, the reason for the break-up of the Soviet Union was definitely mass agoraphobia . . .'

It is that kind of scintillating remark which has our Phobic Fool avoiding non-loons, preferring to gather with other crazies who, like him, are of the firm belief that there are few more interesting things to do at dinner parties than compare neuroses and phobias:

'Yes, I'm agoraphobic too, but mine is complicated by a fear of large women who resemble my boss.'

Our sample Phobic Fool has collected an enviable array of anxieties. Why, he is almost singlehandedly rewriting standard texts on the subject! Let us examine a few:

CLAUSTROLEECHPHOBIA: His anxiety of being in enclosed spaces because he might be attacked by blood-sucking leeches.

AGOROCRANIALCRAPHOBIA: His fear of being outdoors because a bird might defecate on his head.

AVIODIMINUMETEORVACUUMOPHOBIA: His avoidance of air travel on the grounds that a small asteroid might hit the plane and suck him out.

DRIBBLYRUNRUNAMPUTATOPHOBIA: His morbid fear of blowing his nose in case it comes off in the handkerchief.

TYPADHESOPHOBIA: His personal veto on using typewriters because there might be super glue on the keys and he'd never get his fingers off.

ELEVATOGODZILLAMATEPHOBIA: His terror of riding in lifts because Godzilla might leap in and try to breed with him.

EGGALIENOPHOBIA: His nausea-causing dread of eating poached eggs because an alien might jump out of the yolk and rip his neck to shreds.

The list unfortunately goes on and on, to the point that, short of spending his life in a tight-fitting body suit made of gladwrap and getting about on a small wooden sled, our Type 3 Ersatz Loon lives his life in a perennially petrified state, and is regarded as the equivalent of the village idiot by his neighbours.

If you, for some obscure reason, nurse the aim of joining the Ersatz Loons' bandwagon to banality, you had better leap aboard quickly. The carriages are already dangerously over-full!

So popular is this form of failure becoming that many Ersatz Loons are trying radically new ways, exploring new obsessions and, in the process, making new friends . . . Like Elvis; or space-creatures who hover above their cars and take them for joy rides; or the paper boy who was Rasputin in a past life; or Christopher Columbus — that nice man who arrives at the bus stop with you. Then there are those who channel multiple personalities: each duller than the last.

Yes, a New Age is dawning for Ersatz Loons, the self-deluded are sailing off into vast new territories, towards a new homeland — 'TERROR INFIRMA'!

So try whichever approach suits you. Remember — it only takes one good phobia, obsession, or neurosis to take you out of the mental mainstream and into the safety zone of Ersatz Loondom!

And how do you judge whether it has worked, this particular Fast-track to Failure? There are some obvious signs:

THE ERSATZ LOON CHECKLIST

1. If, as you talk to your psychiatrist, he pulls large volumes from his bookcase and leafs through them feverishly, there is a good chance he thinks you are a unique form of madman.

2. Look carefully for a hopeful glint in your psychiatrist's eyes when he asks whether you have ever considered suicide. Or when he talks about the virtues of frontal lobotomy.

3. And, finally, test the professional oath your psychiatrist took vowing to keep dangerous lunatics like you off the streets by informing him that you have no health insurance.

But no matter how convincing you are, you will soon come to realise the true nature of the failure associated with seeking psychiatric help. Sooner or later all Ersatz Loons come to the crushing realisation that there is no excuse — you are not mad.

You are simply a loser.

Chemical Dependence and You

Chapter 11

*T*he drunk, the lush, the soak. Every family should have one! They're better than television, funnier than films. Of course there are many forms of chemical dependence one can turn to in the quest for instantaneous and profound failure — or at least a sense of it — but there is nothing quite like alcohol to magnify one's miseries and bind together life's other disparate grey threads. Let us look through the glass darkly and isolate the divisions of dipsomania.

There are five basic drunk-types which (as most drunks have only the most basic grasp of the English language) we will call Types A, B, C, D and E. Use the following quiz to determine which drunk type you are, and what you are doing wrong in your quest to become a slobbering fool.

Determining Your Drunk Type

1. On first becoming drunk do you:

Type A: Begin to feel much more interesting?

Type B: Begin to feel much bigger?

Type C: Begin to feel much more artistic?

Type D: Begin to feel much funnier?

Type E: Begin to feel much more sexually attractive?

2. On drinking another glass, do you:

Type A: Feel more interesting than anyone else at the party?

Type B: Feel huge, and imagine you hear the sounds of tearing clothes — your own — as you sense your muscles burst forth, unchecked?

Type C: Feel lines of haiku poetry jostle in your mind together with interior decorating ideas and movie soundtracks?

Type D: Feel hilarious, and begin chuckling before you tell a joke?

Type E: Feel yourself?

3. By the middle of the night do you:

Type A: Hold forth on why the problems with the Big Bang theory of the universe do not negate the possibility of a horseshoe-shaped galaxy . . . or necessarily mean the moon was once an atoll in the Pacific Ocean . . . or prove undeniably that a Black Hole the size of a pin once rammed into a Siberian forest?

Type B: Purposely bump into people and growl, before pushing them out of your way; realising that everyone is out to get you, or is simply stupid, or is both, but in any case definitely deserves a taste of your iron fists and an exhibition of your primary school boxing skills?

Type C: Expound on the fact that you have developed a totally new art form which involves inscribing your haiku poetry on walls, carpet, and lounge furniture, while the poems are recited from speakers hidden around the room to the backing of your concerto for ocarina?

Type D: Remember jokes you told in previous lives and laugh hysterically before and after you tell a joke . . . often neglecting to even tell the joke, just laughing and having the world laugh with you (God, you are funny — if you only had a tape recorder running, you think, as you laugh and laugh and laugh. And look at them all, don't they all wish they were as funny as me. Hah, hah, hah, hah, hah, hah, hah!)?

Type E (Men): Nurse what must be the largest erection in the room, your hand thrust manfully into your pocket to try to disguise your largeness so the other men don't feel insignificant and so their wives and girlfriends don't rush from them to you screaming and tearing their clothes off (you nevertheless know what the women are thinking and brush your impaling manhood against them while running your fingers down their backs in that unique way you know will have their fantasies running riot (so maybe not at this party, but on a quiet afternoon sometime they will be unable to control themselves and will call you from their office and discuss what they would like to do to you, and you'll meet that night and you won't say a word — it will all be understood between the two of you that it is something she *has* to do and has *had* to do since she saw you that night; you will make love while the rain thunders outside and she will scream with pleasure and the room will reverberate around you until her screams become whimpers, and she drives her nails into your back and whispers that she never had it so good!))?

Type E (Women): Sashay, catlike, through the adoring glances, feeling them undress you and knowing what those men are thinking, attached to their mousy wives and girlfriends, as your breasts heave, thrusting outwards in that wonderfully self-supporting way (you know that Enrique will leave that bitch soon and he will come to you all apologetic, but you will find it in your heart to accept him as you lead him to your room and he massages your scalp and rubs your back with perfumed oil; it will rain outside as he makes love to you, and all those years of frustration within him will well up and overflow, as he realises it is you he has really wanted all this time — he will weep uncontrollably and you will hold him to your thrusting, wonderfully self-supporting breasts and forgive him in an ecstatic moment of passion!)?

4. By the end of the night do you:

Type A: Attempt to enunciate the incredibly interesting things whirling around in your head, but find that when you open your mouth your tongue cringes back into your throat and makes you want to vomit?

Type B: Still bump into people, furious and wanting to punch them because they are between you and the backyard where you have to vomit 'cause one of them spiked your drinks purposely to get you drunk so you wouldn't be able to beat the living shit out of them . . . but tomorrow is another day isn't it . . . Aarrggh!?

Type C: Repaint the outside walls in an expressionist fashion with the contents of your stomach while humming 'Ode to a Brush Turkey' as would be recited by a brush turkey — aargh, aaargh, gobbleaargh!?

Type D: Cackle uproariously as you career towards the back lawn: hah, hah, hah, hah, hah, hah, hah, haaarrrggghhh! haaarrrggghhh! haaarrrggghhh! haaarrrggghhh!?

Type E: Find that your nether regions are still aflame, still needing satisfaction and, yes, you could still make love now! but it would be nicer if you could just rid yourself of that gurgling, bubbling, swishing, swilling sensation going on just above your nether regions . . . washing, swashing, gurgle, burble, pop . . . Aaarrgggh!?

5. In the morning, is the reality of yourself which faces you:

Type A: Very dull?
Type B: Very small?
Type C: Functionally illiterate?
Type D: Very funny?
Type E (Men): Shrunken and hanging loosely like a small pendulum?
Type E (Women): Shrunken and hanging loosely like small pendulums?

Obviously any one of these categories is custom-made for failure, but try mixing them up. Experiment with various complementary chemicals. Smoking, for example, is a great enhancer for any inebriation session — coupling the multifarious miseries of drunkenness with the sensation of having your mouth attached to the 'blow' orifice of a vacuum cleaner from a homeless men's shelter.

Achieving complete and overall failure in life through one strategy is a rare feat, but a not unrealistic aim when it comes to chemical dependence. Of course you will have to work at it. Irreversible moral and motor function decay doesn't come easy; there are lessons to be learnt along the way — the art of shaving your tongue; living with self-loathing; how to exist four days in the same underwear; etc.

And most importantly, if you decide to embark on this road to ruin, don't drink the good stuff! As a friend of mine said before the operation:

'Drink cheap, drink twice!'

Don't worry, a cigarette will always take the taste away.

Part V

HIGH FINANCE FAILURE

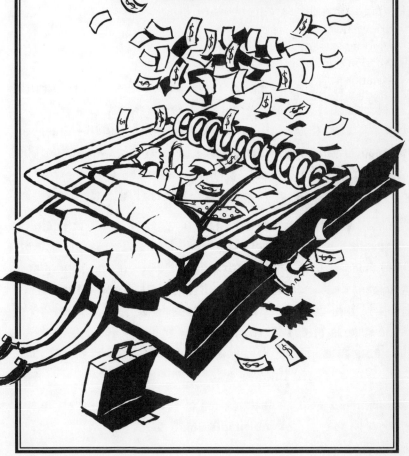

Incredibly Bad Investment Ideas

Chapter 12

*T*he lure of the quick buck. The one good idea. The investment so astute it almost guarantees a corporate jet as a fringe benefit. Yes, almost all authentic Fast-track Failures dream of the road to Eldorado at some stage in their downward slide. And the secret is that almost anyone can come up with a success-proof investment idea — it really isn't all that hard!

The ability to lose money is innate in most of us — it is simply a question of the amount. Like anything, divesting yourself of vast sums of cash and assuring yourself of lifelong penury and immense debt requires application and hard work. The Fast-track Failure can — with a little experience — learn the art of the reverse-Midas touch. While you may not have had a bad business idea in your life, you may nevertheless be closer than you think to utter financial ruin.

Let us begin with an examination of the misery to be made out of the simple credit card.

Credit — The Main Squeeze

On the learning curve to zero liquidity, the ability to mishandle credit is an important lesson. You should currently possess about eighteen credit cards. Determined to use the System, you previously had twelve. Then the System realised you were one of those It dreams about and wrote back to you, offering you another six cards.

As you ran up impossible levels of personal debt, and suspecting you were a wilful abuser of credit cards and would probably at some stage have to mortgage everything to pay them off, the System, in the shape of a credit card company, wrote you a letter which began:

'Dear Valued Cardholder . . .'

and went on:

'Understanding, as we do, that occasionally our Valued Cardholders experience a temporary lack of liquidity, we are willing to offer you an extension of your credit facility, subject only to our nominal interest charge of 35% . . .'

Note: If at this stage you paid off and cancelled your cards, you would receive a letter like this from the credit card company:

'Dear Potential Valued Cardholder . . .'
'Isn't it about time you grew up and got a credit card like every other fully functioning, normal, well-adjusted individual?'

But of course you don't cancel your cards, do you? A credit card is like hot and cold running water: it's a necessity!

ISN'T IT?

All great businessmen use debt, why not you?

It is at about this time in your financial slide (when you attempt to withdraw money from an automatic teller and its screen lights up inviting you to play 'Space Invaders') that you decide to find a way out of your dilemma. A business plan, an audacious investment.

A better mouse trap!

But how? What do you know about business acumen? You, who thought 'acumen' was found in eggs!

Most Fast-track Financial Failures attempt to learn the secrets of success from others who claim to know them. In other words, by . . .

Becoming a Seminar Junkie

The Financial Flop often spends thousands of dollars on self-help books and seminars on how to succeed. Indeed, it is a prerequisite for business failure that one attend at least three 'How to Succeed' seminars. Most often they are run by small men with large accents and wallets bulging with your money.

But how does one approach a 'How to Succeed' seminar?

Firstly, don't be embarrassed! Remember, everyone else there, apart from the small man with the large accent, is by definition a failure like you.

The second most important thing you must do is suspend disbelief at the door. Nothing you are about to hear is remotely true, either about the business fortune of the small man with the large accent, or about the potential locked inside your mind.

Especially about the potential locked inside your mind.

The common or garden variety 'How to Succeed' seminar is a dialogue between the small man with the large accent who has found the secret of success (known as the 'fleecer') and those who have not, like you (the 'fleecees').

'All you have to do is go out there and GRAB IT!'

shouts the small man with the large accent.
('*Grab it?*' You wonder . . .)

'You have nothing to fear except fear itself!'

howls the man, with immense inflection, as he duck-walks across the stage like Chuck Berry in thongs.

('*But I'm terrified of fear,*' you think.)

'If I had a dollar for everyone who leaves one of these seminars and becomes a success, I'd be a rich man!'

His duck-walk briefly becomes a '60s go-go dance before he arches over into a limbo, bent double by his massive accent.

('*But I paid a hundred dollars already to come here as a failure,*' you whisper . . .)

'You know — I used to be like you . . . now look at me! I have It and you don't!'

He rotates on his back like a fly dying and his accent reaches fever pitch.

('"*It*" *definitely has something to do with accents,*' you decide belatedly.)

'So go, conquer! Go and Grab that Thing and never let It go!'

The little man pounds his accent out of his chest with clenched fists and finally, missing his chest, punches himself in the head and keels over with a final 'Grab It!'

('*More grabbing?*' You think. '*So It is all about grabbing and accents? Of course!*')

'OF COURSE!!!' You experience a crystalline moment of pure realisation, crushing in its clarity. Opportunity grips you by the throat. 'OF COURSE!!!'

As you leave the small man crumpled on stage instinctively fingering your money in his pockets, and join the other hundred or so would-be-tycoons shuffling out of the auditorium (some of whom have already begun Grabbing the Thing), you wonder at how simple it all seems now.

The crowd of may-be-magnates and moguls is abuzz with a generic accent which sounds something like that of a Pakistani who grew up in New York but who now lives in South Africa.

'Let's go and grab it!'

you murmur to your neighbour with a heavily accented murmur.

'Yes!'

comes the hushed, accented reply.

Deciding you don't want to rush things too much and that you can just as easily become a baron of industry in the morning, you go home and try out your new power accent on your children and your wife. As you expound upon 'Grabbing' and outline your strategy for world financial domination, they stare silently at you across the chops and vegetables before your wife breaks the impasse:

'Darling, please don't be an idiot at the dinner table. It disturbs the children . . .'

And you begin to make excuses in your mind as to what you really did with that hundred dollars!

Eventually you spend so much trying to learn how to succeed that you fail through lack of money.

You begin to question whether you will *ever* be rich beyond your wildest dreams. The answer is quite simple.

No.

But that won't stop you trying, will it? You — you who have nothing! You will not be satisfied until you come up with a fool-proof business plan — and then realise that, being a fool, you are prevented from going any further with it.

Timing is Everything

Coming up with a money-making idea depends first on timing: picking the right product for the right market at the right time. And the converse is true — doomed business strategies must be exquisitely timed for their failure to be assured.

Simple is often best. Start with a small bad idea which you can build from, like going into a joint venture with your in-laws just before your divorce, or buying shares in a whaling company because they're cheap at the moment.

When you finally get serious, you must write out a business plan, a statement of intent about your corporate future. If it looks as silly on paper as it does in your mind, you may be deterred from going on. But if — by reading it in the dark or squinting a lot — your business plan still appears to make sense, you must take it to your bank manager (preferably at night during an electricity strike, or failing that at least on an overcast day).

In any other culture the jottings which make up business plans would be dismissed as the megalomanic ramblings of a loon. In our culture, however, they are taken most seriously, and often — as in your case — large sums of money are lent on the basis of a couple of pages of delusional thinking.

Begin by borrowing lots and lots of money. Then borrow more money.

Then begin spending it.

The first thing you will realise about your business plan is that the bits in it with numbers next to them are completely untrue. Not a little off. Utterly off! Like the quote for interior decorating, or the cost of stock, transport and provision for damage, wastage and theft.

UTTERLY OFF!

After a month of being operational you have two options:

---

1. Cry a great deal — wail and gnash your teeth.

or:

2. Borrow lots more money.

You decide there is something untidy about a would-be tycoon wailing and gnashing his teeth, so you borrow lots more money.

Then one day, apropos of absolutely nothing and certainly nothing to do with your current line of failure, it hits you.

The one good idea!

It is a pity that even now, yours will be . . .

An Embarrassing Success

Some people have the knack of taking business success and making it *look* like failure. It turns out you are one of those sorts of people.

Surprise, surprise.

There is no real way of learning how to be an Embarrassing Success Story — it requires extraordinarily lateral thinking, an art which cannot be taught (though lying on the footpath sometimes produces the odd halfway good idea, and at the very least people throw coins at you).

No, the Embarrassing Success looks at a situation in a way no-one else has.

The situation is usually in the area of personal hygiene.

It is worth quoting some illustrations of Embarrassing Success Stories at this juncture. Perhaps the classic examples are those people who have made millions from inventing an innovative nostril hair trimmer, or come up with an ingenious ear-wax flushing system.

Great successes!

It's just that no one wants to talk to them. When questions about the source of their wealth arise at the few dinner parties they are invited to, another guest will normally pipe up:

'Please, not while we're eating.'

Voila — embarrassing success!

But we have forgotten you (a dangerously easy thing to do).

What *is* this imaginative fulcrum on which the rest of your life balances?

Is it an electric toe scraper, or a musical dental floss dispenser? No!

Your vision splendid is . . .

A HOME HAIR TRANSPLANT SYSTEM!

Already you can hear the advertising jingle:

'You take a hair from there,
And you put it here . . .
From under your arms,
Behind your palms . . .
What's left on the bed,
Will end up on your head . . .
With new HAIRSHIFT!'

Billboards across the country will blare:

'DON'T SHAVE . . . TRANSPLANT!'

Yes — you will be a revolutionary in the hair transplant industry!

Thus, as with everything, eventually — even if you succeed — you fail.

FAILURE IN SPORT AND RECREATION

Exercise — All Pain, No Gain

Chapter 13

Thus far we have been almost exclusively discussing the breakdown of spiritual fibre, the crumbling of the mind and destruction of the faculty of independent thought. Now we will apply the same Stalinist principles to your body as yet another way of Fast-tracking to Failure.

You may have already observed Sporting Failures. They slouch into work looking as if their body woke up half an hour after their mind; they tell you they are too weak to have sex; they have raging athlete's foot from the locker room showers; they are reduced to crawling as a form of exercise. Muscle fibre has turned into jelly. Their bodies have simply said 'No way, Jose!'

What happened?

They tried to get fit.

Man's imagination is boundless when it comes to mishandling his body in a manner utterly unrelated to wage earning, but we will try to cover the main areas of what we, in the business of applied futility, call Exercomania. In an effort to outline this broadly successful method of misery, we will look at the main sub-groups of Exercomaniacs.

The Fashion Freak:
How to Become Exercomaniac Type 1

Any exercise actually performed by this species of sweater is only by default, for the name of the primary game is fashion. These types are easily spotted by the well-trained observer of failure: prowling around gyms in leopard-skin leotards, hair wonderfully coiffed or gelled. You will notice a mirror is always within close range. (That is how one can differentiate Fashion Freaks from people who simply like to hang around gymnasiums.)

In order to become a Fashion Freak, you must ensure that when you do exercise, the emphasis is purely on style. Aerobics are a popular choice: for women they provide the opportunity for exaggerated arm movements and wrist flicks, and well-practised facial expressions of determination which highlight those fine eyebrows and bone structure, all carefully performed to minimise sweat stains and maximise the image of a svelte sex kitten sheathed only in a metallic paint job. Men tend to stalk about aerobics classes and gymnasiums like black panthers, with a bolt of silver lycra accenting their extremely fit-looking protuberance.

When not performing some form of exertion to music which seems to have been exclusively composed to sweat to, you should choose an exercise regimen in the vanguard of vogue — the workout system of the stars. Recent examples include stair-climbing machines, water aerobics, and exercising while hanging upside down.

Adopting such a workout system allows new heights of failure to be achieved, as a common or garden variety Fashion Freak often overlooks one small fact.

Stars own their own gymnasiums and can lock the doors.

You see, most of these new-wave exercises, while possibly quite effective, look extremely silly . . .

THE FOOTPATH FASHION FREAK

These sub-species of Fashion Freaks take their show on the road — jogging in the very latest all-weather spandex with matching headband, and shoes bedecked with expensive looking straps, swellings and written instructions.

As a Footpath Fashion Freak you can offer a fine sight indeed: knees nice and high, elbows tucked in, nose angled to optimise air intake — all the while maintaining a blissful self-awareness of how you look to passersby — a lean road machine as chic and sleek as a Concorde in a wind tunnel.

If you encounter another Fashion Freak on the road, the salutation between you two seraphs should be a studious indifference to the pain associated with your triumph over the laws of gravity, and instead an expression of deep contemplation which suggests you must both be extremely important people when not jogging.

Both public humiliation and intense pain can be achieved by Fashion Freaks exercising in this exterior manner.

The Benefits of Being a Footpath Fashion Freak

1. The overall effect you create while jogging less resembles a supersonic aircraft in flight, and rather more so a pelican with chewing gum on its feet.

2. This form of exercise offers an unlimited opportunity of running into inanimate objects. One's concentration on maintaining style, and conviction in one's self image, must be complete for this result, but when all the pieces come together, there is nothing quite as glorious as a Voguish One, his eyes on the eyes on him, jogging majestically into a set of traffic lights, or a 'No Standing' sign or, occasionally, a monument or statue.

In the end the quintessential failure of the Fashion Freak is much more than the chance to run into inanimate objects or become a thing of public ridicule — it is the delusion of achieving good health when in reality more actual exercise would be achieved by alternating hands when using teabags!

Which would *never* happen to . . .

The Serious Jogger:
How to Become Exercomaniac Type 2

The Serious Jogger eats Fashion Freaks for breakfast. When you encounter such scum — mostly during the last two hours of your daily marathon — you do your best to imitate an oncoming road sign. Fashion Freaks are nothing more than impediments to a Serious Jogger, and the frustration which can build up in you by being stuck behind one of these high-stepping fools often requires jogging an additional ten miles to overcome.

A Serious Jogger has run in the same clothes for the past ten years; sweat has eaten much of them away and their odour precedes you by a couple of days. Your headband has left an almost visible indentation in your skull. The mode of communication between Serious Joggers en route should be a low grunt followed by a lowering of the head (it is, by the way, the mode of communication most Serious Joggers adopt during the rest of the day as well).

As a Serious Jogger you took your first steps and uttered your first grunts about ten years ago. Since then you have increased your mileage daily, and long past are the big decisions the truly Serious Jogger must make to become proficient at profound perambulation.

The biggest decision faced by the Serious Jogger is:

'In which direction to run?'

This decision is doubly difficult when the running track is circular or oval. The angst which can go into clockwise or anti-clockwise is incredible. A Serious Jogger will normally agonise over this quandary for some time, plotting the onward flow of humanity, the preferred direction of those damn nancy-boys and girls in their flashy clothes, and the route taken by the shuffling relics who have risen to the high priesthood of profound perambulation.

Finally you decide —

'Clockwise!'

Living with the consequences of a decision of such magnitude is not easy — it normally takes some weeks to settle into it, and cast off those nagging doubts that the wind assistance may have been different had you chosen counter-clockwise. But with each Fashion Freak you oppose and elbow jab, and each relic you pass and grunt to, a Serious Jogger becomes more and more satisfied with clockwise, able eventually even to share your decision with your family and workmates. Finally, those who do run counter-clockwise become non-people, genetic cripples who made the wrong choice and now must pay for it. There is no sympathy in the mind of the Serious Jogger for these unfortunates.

> **I**t is a brutal, grunting world out there — you wear your runners and you take your chances.

However, rather than achieving Olympian health, a Serious Jogger is more often on the fast track to complete bodily failure. Joints are usually the first to go: toes, knees, hips, spine, shoulders — a kind of creeping paralysis which at some time or other reduces you to a shuffling shadow of your former self. But still you jog on!

The next area of physical degeneration usually occurs in the muscles, and before too long the only flesh responding to aerobic stimulus is the Serious Jogger's gums. For a while your tongue flails weakly in your mouth, but then you completely lose the faculty of coherent speech. And finally the brain simply burns out at a certain point . . . Still you jog, a primitive reflex arc without reference to its environment; jogging, jogging, jogging . . .

But — even on your good days — the Serious Jogger *accomplishes* nothing, a waste of effort according to . . .

The Practical Performer:
How to Become Exercomaniac Type 3

This form of get-fit failure works out by maximising the effort involved with day-to-day activities and household chores. Who needs a power mower when a push-mower (or even a pair of garden shears) will do the same job with twice the effort? Practical Performers look at every situation with a view to optimising its exercise potential: using teabags; whipping cream; sawing wood; beating carpets; shaving.

Recently, one Practical Performer was spotted working up a sweat doing embroidery.

For the Practical Performer, getting to work occupies much wasted time which could be spent exercising. The first area many concentrate on is finding commuter methods which can combine serious exercise. The simplest of these include:

- ☞ using wrist-strengtheners on the bus
- ☞ performing chin-ups on the hand straps in the tram
- ☞ gripping the steering wheel firmly in peak-hour traffic, while rocking backwards and forwards to tone the shoulders and lower back;

and

- ☞ exercising facial muscles on the rush-hour train.

This last technique — an aerobically designed series of facial contortions — is a particularly efficient use of any time when the rest of the body is forced to be static: in dentists' waiting rooms, in the boss's office, or at restaurants.

More ingenious Practical Performers eschew traditional commuter transport and develop high-strain methods of conveying themselves to work. This began with extremely dangerous, but at least conventional, means like cycling, roller-skating, and even walking! But lately, highly motivated Practical Performers have been seen commuting on grass skis and pogo-sticks.

No life area is exempt from the Practical Performer.

Sex, for example, is a perfect opportunity to combine a good exercise regimen with an everyday act. The missionary position with fifty push-ups is a favourite; and sit-ups, chin-ups, and jogging-on-the-spot can also be used inventively by the sexual athlete. Finally, performing facial exercises while counting to twenty during orgasm will ensure the proper aerobic benefit and blood flow is gained.

Shopping is another area where effort can be increased with no effect on the job at hand. Simply picking the wrong supermarket trolley can give you a work-out you would have to pay good money for at a gym!

Become a mall trekker.

Exercise when cooking! As an example, try mashing the potatoes before you cook them. Mincing meat by hand is also an old favourite.

In the end, with dutiful application and the attitude of never letting a minute pass which could be used to build muscle tone, the day becomes so exhausting, so utterly enervating, that Life itself becomes simply too hard. In this way a Practical Performer can achieve the ultimate failure —

the inability to do anything for fear it will tire you out.

But physical exhaustion is a problem almost never faced by . . .

The Mirror Gazer (Or The Very Fit Nerd):
How to Become Exercomaniac Type 4

To become a successful Mirror Gazer, you must first generate an obsession with a specific muscle, which you then exercise to the exclusion of all others. Some use weights to develop incredibly powerful fingers or toes, others build massive ankles or necks. Women Mirror Gazers seem to concentrate on forms of exercise which take weight exclusively off their chests.

But as Mirror Gazers are almost as common as Fashion Freaks, you must be imaginative. Try, for example, to develop the strongest blink in the gymnasium, lips which could take the top off a beer bottle, or a tongue which can bend cutlery.

The Nirvana for a Mirror Gazer is to develop a single muscle which can pop up on demand, for, as the name implies, there is nothing a Mirror Gazer likes to do more on a free afternoon than hang around the gym's mirror and continually pop his or her muscle for the adulation of spectators.

So where is the failure, I hear you cry?

Well, unfortunately Mirror Gazers so over-develop specific muscles they come to resemble cancerous growths which, when coupled with the neglect the rest of their body suffers as a result of their tunnel-vision exercise regimen, produces the effect of a terminal patient with delusions of fitness.

Which would never happen to . . .

People Who Just Like Hanging Around Gymnasiums:
How to Become Exercomaniac Type 5

This large group are generally troublemakers, failures who are obviously never going to get fit, but who — because of a lack of friends, or because they have nothing else to do except go home and examine their collection of West African stamps — like loitering around women's aerobic classes or leaning against weight machines.

People Who Just Like Hanging Around Gymnasiums usually have specific interests. Some are Sauna Sitters, remaining in there for hours trying to make conversation with those passing through, usually unsuccessfully as they are generally scratching some body part at the time. Others are Spa Soakers, human teabags who are universally despised because they always seem to be wearing bandaids.

But most, usually resplendent in grubby white singlets, are Equipment Fondlers — never actually doing any exercise, but whiling away hours touching the gymnasium weight machines as if a serious workout is imminent.

Which of course it isn't!

The failure of People Who Just Like Hanging Around Gymnasiums is obvious, but passive.

To be a true Fast-track Flop you must, as is stressed time and time again in this field guide to failure, seize destiny by the bootstraps and play an active part in your own undoing.

And others must witness your decline – which never happens to . . .

The Video Devotee:
How to Become Exercomaniac Type 6

As this form of exercise fanatic plays out their failure in private, we will deal with it cursorily.

The home of a Video Devotee centres, not surprisingly, around a large television. The television is framed on either side by other discarded tools of home exercise, most usually the following: an exercise bike, a Charles Atlas bull-worker, various plastic devices which once claimed to 'tighten thighs in only five minutes a day', a home rowing machine, and a plethora of elastic straps attached to the walls. On top of the television is a stack of video cassettes with impossibly fit looking movie stars on their covers.

The basic trick to being a Video Devotee is maximising the difference between yourself and the impossibly fit looking movie star prancing around on-screen. Wearing one's underwear while exercising is a good starting point. You should also exercise while gripping the video player's remote control so you can rewind any bits you miss.

Choosing exercise videos which concentrate on dancing puts you ahead of the pack — as these exercises involve not only shuffling your grossly unfit body around your living room, **BUT DOING IT IN RHYTHM!** You then double your chances of failing and certainly enhance your exclusion from the 'beautiful' set.

In the end, embarrassing yourself in private has only limited benefits for the dedicated loser — it is far better to concentrate on becoming an object of public ridicule. But if you insist on performing like a fool at home, at least leave the curtains open.

Misery and the Arts

(Or How to Alienate Very Dangerous Groups of People)

Chapter 14

*I*t is often thought by those who are despondent that a way of dragging themselves out of their condition is to write the great Australian novel, symphony or screenplay, or at least conceive a new birthday card greeting. Unfortunately, the only route the arts open up to the downcast is the road to abject misery. But if you are determined to subject others to bad art and yourself to scorn, there are well-tried methods for circumventing the usual obstacles to failure in the arts — poetic pleasure, moral uplifting, a sense of moment, inspiration, a place in history.

The first hindrance in the quest for artistic non-achievement in any area is the concept of inspiration — those moments when you feel truly righteous about yourself and your abilities. Most often the dizzy feeling would-be artists feel, the sense of well-being, the notion that you may actually be creating something, is as potentially artistic as a room full of chimpanzees with a word processor.

Before you can go on you must realise that inspiration can be one of many things:

Probable Causes of Inspirational Feelings

1. A lack of food.

2. A profound excess, or absence, of alcohol.

3. High blood pressure.

4. An imminent stroke.

5. The impact of the bullet fired by the extremist group you have enraged with your art.

If you can convince yourself that 'inspiration' is the result of dangerously high blood pressure, and likely as not you will die before completing the dedication to your great novel, you will quickly move on to a less circuitous path to self-degradation.

If your 'inspirational' dizziness is, in fact, an imminent stroke, then there is not much you can really do about it unfortunately. But at least try to die with indignity — moan a lot, thrash about, cause yourself added pain. If it turns out not to be a stroke after all, nothing has been lost — death will happen to you sooner or later, and a dry run is not a bad idea.

However, if your capacity for self-delusion is boundless, and you believe you can fashion a work of art so worthy as to be sent on the next inter-stellar space probe as an example of the cultural heights reached by the civilisation of homo sapiens, then brace yourself for a major let down.

Especially if art really *does* imitate Life.

BECOMING UNREAD

Insistent on embarking on your foolhardy direction, you must now choose a topic about which your art will be created. It is important that your topic be of no interest to the rest of humanity, and only of fleeting interest to you. For example, you could decide to:

☞ Write bad poetry about chickens, or songs about cottage cheese.

☞ After the success of movies like *Terminator*, pen a screenplay based on a killer cow or a psychotic philosopher called *Ruminator*.

☞ Write a concerto for an unplayed instrument, eg 'Concerto in A Flat for Orchestra and Small Amazonian Bamboo Pipe'. Or music which takes as its inspiration an utterly worthless activity, like 'Music to Floss Your Teeth By'.

But worst of all, write about yourself. You would not have reached the latter stages of this book unless you were a particularly loathsome and frightfully uninteresting specimen of sentient existence, whose life has as much interest for the reading public as the workings of a cockroach trap.

It is the first law of writing that you write about your own experiences.

Actually, that is the second law of writing.

The first law is that you can, in fact, write, and that is the major assumption being made here.

Write about your miserable childhood; your distressing school days; your repulsion of all members of the opposite sex, which limited itself not only to your own species, but most of the warm-blooded world; your failures at college; and your experiences at work. Real life experiences which begin:

☞ 'Our eyes met across the water cooler . . .'

☞ 'As I sensuously slid my ledger into her accounts payable tray I knew . . .'

☞ 'It was something about the way my boss was treading on my head that gave me the first clue that something was wrong . . .'

☞ 'It was seeing her brand of cereal at the checkout that gave me hope . . .'

☞ 'The way he pushed "3" on the elevator was meant as a secret message for my eyes only . . .'

Another well-used method is 'Miserable Minimalism' — writing a novel of many hundreds of pages that takes place solely in one location. A book with the title of:

- ☞ **Alone on the Toilet.**
- ☞ **Views from my Desk.**
- ☞ **Reflections in the Computer Terminal.**
- ☞ **From Here to the Next Room and Back.**
- ☞ **All About Freeze-dried Coffee.**

You can write biographies of utterly uninteresting historical figures such as:

- ☞ **Napoleon's Dry-cleaner.**
- ☞ **The Man Who Nearly Invented Electricity First.**

and

- ☞ **The Fifth Person to Reach the North Pole.**

Or look at titles which have been successful before and modify them. For example, following on from *Confessions of an Opium Eater*:

- ☞ **Confessions of a Cigarette Chewer.**

and others:

- ☞ **Nail Polish Remover and Me.**
- ☞ **Zen and the Art of Egg Frying.**

Take an unpopular pursuit and glamorise it:

- ☞ **Warren the Whale Hunter.**
- ☞ **The Joy of Ivory Poaching.**
- ☞ **A Communist Future.**

Be gripped by love and write hideous haiku poetry:

'You set off an H-bomb in me, and
like a dove you fly,
Through the nuclear fallout of my mind.'

LITERARY TOOLS FOR FOOLS

Much can be achieved by the inappropriate use of literary tools. For example:

Create a science fiction epic so complex that the glossary of pseudo-jargon is as long as the book:

'When Zyphic Otoc called Mut with his Sygonic Implement on his home planet of Craxis in the galactic cloud of Gartimus, he explained that his Asogynist Mass Carpathicor had sprung a leak in its Hyposlot. Mut sent word through a passing Ygonnor that Emperor Zalgred had requested Zyphic to attend the Annual Bumdercryx and was sending a Zone Relocator for that purpose.'

Or achieve much the same in the traditional literary form by overusing your thesaurus:

'Precipitation descended on Harold as he premeditated his next machination. The acclivity up which he gallivanted brought recollection from his abdicory of the Roman abatis. His nose, already ablated by the luminous celestial body around which the Earth revolves, inhaled the redolence of the passionless herbage.'

(Translation: It was raining as Harry wondered what to do next. The hill he was climbing was like a bloody fort and his sunburnt nose copped a whiff of something nasty.)

Or use a foreign language, like Latin or Ancient Greek, without translation, in the pretentious assumption that your readers have a conversational ability in all the dialects on Earth.

This babel-like approach is particularly effective in detective thrillers:

'Thrust Carr stopped, his grubby fingers gripping the handle of his Smith and Wesson. The bullets gone, he had but one chance and he meant to take it: "Semper in excreta. Macte nova virtute, peur," he muttered, the Latin he had learnt in the Jesuit school when studying for the priesthood coming back effortlessly. *"Sic itur ad astra"*, he murmured and then struck. The sound of smashing skull tore the night like a garbage compactor.'

This technique is also interesting when used in western novels:

'Black Bart held the mane of the fiery pinto. The mountain stretched before him; behind was the rumbling posse of Sheriff Max. The dry Nevada air never smelt so good as it did now and he wanted to keep smelling it — after all, hadn't Pythagoras said "φιλοκαλουμεν τε γαρ μετ ευτειας και φιλοσφουμεν αυευ μαλακιας"? Bart swallowed hard and galloped. He knew the route he was taking was the square of the value of the hypotenuse of his pursuers', and he stood a good chance of getting back to Sweet Lorraine.'

Beginning each chapter of your turgid tome, utterly devoid of any literary merit, with a classical quote in a transparent attempt to elevate its tone is also a futile literary tool:

' *Mine eye hath played the painter and hath stelled,*
Thy beauty's form in table of my heart,
My body is the frame wherein 'tis held . . .'
(Shakespeare, Sonnet 24)

I gripped her upper thigh and ran my fingers under the beginnings of her underwear. She shuddered, wanting me at that moment more than she wanted her underwear . . .'

Come up with grossly inappropriate phrases for describing genitalia and the sex act:

'She saw his iridescent impaler, perpendicular priest to the religion of love, rise before her like a time-lapse asparagus. Her valley of yearning throbbed like a fresh football injury and her thighs tightened like soft chopsticks. His ballooning manhood thrashed within her like a dolphin dying in a drift net and finally fired like an umbilical uzi. He came towards her like a head-on collision, and she held him like a locked inertial seatbelt.'

Writing while under the influence of alcohol or any other addictive chemical is extremely important to unimaginative writing:

> **'He ran towards her . . . faster and faster and faster and faster and faster and faster and faster. She ran fast too. He ran even faster. She ran towards him, fast. Fast, he ran towards her. Him, she ran fast towards. He and she ran fast towards each other. They both ran faster and faster and faster.'**

It is incredible what you can convince yourself is good writing through a chemical fog filter. But drugs, like alcohol, serve another useful purpose — the eradication of inspiration. As an artistic also-ran once said:

> **'Creating nothing unique is one percent inspiration and ninety-nine percent proof.'**

Try it — after a while you will be amazed at how little you can get done when you really try. (See Chapter 11 — Chemical Dependence and You.)

But perhaps one of the quickest and most permanent techniques for achieving complete misery and alienation from society is by enraging a major extremist group with your art. Ascribe a weird sexual perversion to the extremist group's god of choice, ridicule a few of their prophets, or describe all of mankind (but particularly the extremist group) as having sprung from the loins of a sex doll.

Or perhaps you should begin your epic by simply writing the words:

'The End'.

Embarrassing Your Pet

Chapter 15

At a certain time in every Fast-track Failure's life, you reach the point at which you have no friends, and the only people who will talk to you are those being paid to do it. It is at about this stage of your decline that you may look to the animal world for companionship and support. And because people who hang around zoos alone frequently attract the attention of authorities, you may well decide your only option is to buy a pet.

Ever since prehistoric times, man's attitude towards his domestic animals has always been to treat them as a form of self-expression. Thus a pet goat came to express 'Rich Man', a pet dog came to suggest 'Man Who Doesn't Chew His Bones Properly' and so on.

And so in his first few faltering steps, man began to stamp his personality on his beasts and began a glorious tradition whereby succeeding generations of losers exacerbated their ignominy by their choice of pet.

There are various techniques of pet ownership the Fast-track Failure can employ.

Being Dominated By Your Pet

This method is far and away the most popular form of pet ownership. It practically guarantees a few more downward steps on the ladder of Life. To be dominated by one's pet involves the first step of buying an assertive pet which can pull it off. (Cases of owners being dominated by their budgies are rare, though it has been achieved in a few spectacular instances.)

Most Pet Submissives opt for a cat or dog, and their pet's dominance begins with the hysterical amount of money shelled over for a small furry thing one twentieth the size of a car! Obviously the dominance being discussed here is of the intellectual or spiritual kind, not the physical. For the latter (including information such as 'How to be savaged by your own dog') contact your local bull terrier owners association.

No, what we are discussing is the intuitive superiority of the pet over its master. Apart from being a highly leveraged debt as mentioned above, the dominant pet wastes no time in establishing its pre-eminence in the household of the Pet Submissive. For example, a favourite training curve of assertive dogs for their masters involves the following:

ASSERTIVE DOG TRAINING CURVE

Step 1. Sleep deprivation of owner — achieved through assertive dog howling, barking, door scratching etc.

Step 2. Inverting owner's body clock to match timing of dog's bodily functions — achieved through assertive dog demanding to relieve itself routinely at 2.00 am.

Step 3. Turning owner into simpering apologist for dog — achieved by assertive dog growling at small children, small dogs and large hairy men.

Step 4. Developing morale-crumbling obsessions in owner — achieved by assertive dog scratching violently and whining whenever owner is in the same room.

Step 5. Embarrassing the owner in public — achieved by assertive dog urinating on occupied cars, attempting to mate with dogs one tenth its size, and attempting to mate with legs of human pedestrians.

Step 6. Destroying all hope of owner having a fulfilling love life — achieved through assertive dog mounting owner's friend at inopportune times, licking cutlery before 'special' dinners, and following owner to bedroom and watching.

In no time at all, having successfully alienated the owner from his fellow Man, the assertive dog is all the owner has left, and that is precisely how the dog wants it. It is little wonder then that submissive owners come to so closely resemble their pets!

With cats and the Pet Submissive owner, it is not so much a matter of spiritual breakdown achieved through the above Manchurian Mutt Method, but complete intellectual supremacy achieved by the cat. The assertive cat simply adopts an attitude of haughty disdain — that same demeanour utilised by humans who *know* they are far, far smarter than the rest of us.

A sideways glance from the assertive cat has its owner changing brands of cat food; a curt swish of the tail is enough to convince the owner he has body odour; a casual nod of the head or lick of the paw assures the vacillating Pet Submissive owner that he *should* leave his job after all. And the reverse ploy is also executed well by assertive cats in their manipulation of Pet Submissives: the odd warm purr, the occasional rub against the leg, the rare lap-sit; all evoke sounds of whimpering gratitude from the owner.

Becoming completely dominated by your pet is perhaps one of the surest methods of achieving complete social alienation and, implicitly, long-term failure. The one drawback is you are left with only your pet to share the glory of your downfall.

I Am My Pet and My Pet is Me

In other fields of human inadequacy this type of individual can be recognised in large cars with 'witty' numberplates like 'Funky', 'Spunky' and 'Romeo', or living in houses with farcical names like 'Nirvana sur Mer', or in discos wearing clothes no self-respecting clown would be caught dead in.

These are people whose self-expression is limited only by what they can buy.

If you decide to follow this path to penury and ridicule, everything you buy must 'say' something about you as an individual.

Including your pet.

In the context of this particular chapter these individuals go by the classification of 'Pet Expressives' (in other chapters the word 'jerk' usually suffices).

The Pet Expressive buys an animal not for its companionship, but as an advertisement for his or her personality:

☞ 'Look at me — what a wild and crazy guy, eh! Who else has a $25,000 macaw to perch on his shoulder while he's supermarket shopping?'

- ☞ 'Look at me — I'm obviously a unique, artistic individual. You can tell that by my having this pigmy pig on a leash!'
- ☞ 'Look at me and die! And when I'm finished enforcing my superior physicality on your puny frame, my bull terrier will complete your progression into hamburger mince!'
- ☞ 'I'm sensitive and frail, I need a man, I need a good romance novel . . . at least I have my chihuahua.'
- ☞ 'I like it . . . a lot. I like doing it. I want to do it to you. Tonight. Over and over. I want to crawl all over your body like my Burmese . . .'

Of course, this can all become a little tricky for many Pet Expressives and the public they are meant to be impressing. With regard to Rottweilers and Great Danes, Persian cats and even pet pigs, it is quite simple to divine what the Pet Expressive is trying to convey about themselves.

But what is the ferret owner trying to disclose to the rest of us?

Or the master of a basset hound?

Or people who keep rats, or fish, or ants?

That is not to say confusion is necessarily a bad thing for someone on the downward curve.

Confusion, remember, breeds contempt.

If the Pet Expressive's mind is so vacuous and the rest of his life so empty that a pet ferret is the extent of his difference, then he is well on the way to being a first-rate failure!

Whichever method you use, remember — we are all simply animals . . . it's just that some of us are higher up the evolutionary ladder than others!

Assessing Your Failure and Failure in the Afterlife

There Are No Easy Answers

(At Least None You Can Understand!)

Chapter 16

It is important at this stage that you have convinced yourself that this is all there is. That there is no hope, things won't get any better, things won't work themselves out.

Things will only take a turn for the worse.

You have failed . . . almost.

To achieve a truly ignominious end you have to firstly take stock of your Earthly failure, and then leave yourself totally unprepared to deal with the Hereafter.

So what of the here and now? How far have you fallen? How little have you achieved? By what increment have you turned back the tide of human progress, what factor of retrograde evolution have you amounted to?

Is the sum total of your life a negative figure?

For an answer, measure yourself against the following profile of a truly successful Fast-track Failure:

The Successful Fast-track Failure

He has not achieved anything. He has no friends except those who treat him as a psychological case study. He has a raging chemical addiction. His spouse wants him back only because she could get a good price for the shoes. His children claim to be adopted and call **'AUSTRALIA'S MOST WANTED'** every time he visits. His boss has recommended him for therapy, his therapist has recommended a lobotomy, his lobotomist has recommended suicide, and his embalmer has recommended a land fill. He has turned to the arts and alienated a large religious group who would take him hostage tomorrow if it wasn't for his breath. Credit card companies have his photograph on posters . . . wanted posters.

But he is not quite utterly miserable . . . so our twilight failure moves to a place he's never lived before, to be with other misfits who think that by moving to a warm climate they will rot more quickly. And, as final proof of his almost complete physical and mental decomposition, he begins to call radio talk-back shows.

So how do you measure up?

Perhaps the question is too hard.

When you put together the good bits and the bad bits of what has happened to you so far, which bits do you have more of?

(a) The bad bits.

(b) The good bits.

If you answered (a), then you are a failure.

If you answered (b), then as a failure you are a failure.

Either way you lose.

The only thing left to do is die with a little indignity.

Choosing the Wrong God

Chapter 17

You have died.

There was no-one at your funeral. The funeral home stole the handles off your coffin. They donated your body to medical science. Medical science sent it back, with a note which said 'thanks all the same, but we're doing just fine with rats'. Your obituary appeared in the second-hand goods section of the newspaper.

The grave digger planted carrots in your plot. The only flowers near your headstone have blown there.

Your headstone is very small. On it is written:

'What a bummer — Derek died.'

or:

'This space for rent.'

or:

'Gravestone kindly donated by Greco's Pizza — for the best pizza in town call Greco's! (PS. Mary has had her last Greco's pizza.)'

and:

'Don't steal the carrots!'

As your soul speeds skyward, you realise the sign at the entrance to your final resting place does not read 'Cemetery', but 'Clean Fill Wanted'.

It is indeed a miserable and ignominious end. But worse is to come.

You hear a booming voice, and are summonsed. You know you are in the presence of the Big One, the Redeemer, the Guy Who Holds All The Cards. The Fellow Who Has A Fondness For Capital Letters When Talking About Him.

And you discover you have chosen the wrong god!

How could this have happened?

You prayed fervently of late, said confession eight times a week, rubbed your rosaries shiny, bowed devotedly towards Mecca, had been a good boy during Passover, worshipped your ancestors in the spirit of Gautama Buddha, and been kind to cows. And what's more, you have *always* voted Liberal!

In short, you are certain that you have grovelled to the Right One!

God speaks:

'**All ye who wish to enter the Kingdom of the Lord must first buy a Rolls Royce Silver Shadow Corniche, together with pastel orange upholstery and red trim. For yea, it is easier for a rich man to enter the Kingdom of Heaven in a 1976 Rolls Royce Silver Shadow Corniche, than for a poor man to ride a camel through the eye of a needle.**'

It is the Bagwan!

You have chosen the wrong god.

And he wants to sell you a car.

Heaven, it seems, is going to be a blur of orange and red, and an endless traffic jam of Rolls Royces.

Then you see that next to the Bagwan is L. Ron Hubbard. And behind him, Sun Myung Moon.

Oh no!

How did you fail to pick that the Kingdom of the Righteous was only open to Orange Moonie Scientologists! What an idiot you have been!

But wait — there is Moses David of the Children of God, and there, levitating for all he is worth, is Maharishi Yogi.

It is Cult Heaven!

Not only did you pick the wrong god, you failed to even get the general religious area right.

'*So this is heaven*?' you wonder.

'*Or perhaps it is simply heaven for failures. Yes, that's it!*' you realise as you see the calibre of the other ghosts surrounding you.

Failure Heaven!

In an odd way this realisation makes you feel better. That is, perhaps, why you are a failure in the first place — having that ability to become relaxed by the sheer act of grasping a situation, regardless of how bad it is.

You are surrounded by a conga line of naked Orange people, and beyond them a larger orbit of Scientology freaks trying desperately to measure your mental resistance (just to assure themselves that it is only failures who have zero mental resistance) and give you a free personality test.

The cultists go on, and on, and on . . . a carnival of failure. That is what is so heavenly — in the absence of someone better to judge yourself by, 'failure' loses its meaning.

This is not so comforting, you decide.

Above it all the Bagwan floats — the only one of the pack who has a sense of humour in heaven. So, always on the lookout for a good joke, you listen to him.

'Listen my Failure Friend,'

he booms, insisting on capitals:

'You have Two Options. Either you Stay Here, buy a Roller and listen to Old Man Hubbard — who's got very Little in the Cupboard and Flowers in the Attic if you Know what I Mean — or you return to Earth and Corporeality, and form a Cult of your Own.'

The Bagwan whispers now:

'Let's drop the formality, and the capitals. The truth is, unfortunately we're getting a bit thin on the ground here in Ersatz Paradise because the fashion's gone right out of pursuing idiotic belief systems on Earth . . .'

But you decide to try out the not-quite-Nirvana for a while, sign up for a monthly payment plan, and drive your 1976 Corniche through the Mikimoto Pearly Gates.

You come to an intersection. On it are signs which read:

'SHOP AROUND FOR YOUR NEXT LIFE!'

and:

'YOU, TOO, CAN BE SHIRLEY MACLAINE!'

and:

'CUSTOMISED REINCARNATIONS THIS WAY!'

As you motor along you realise there is no other traffic, and no pedestrians. Heaven, apparently, means never having to shout at your fellow angel!

But the 1976 Corniche will not go over sixty kilometres per hour. You own the road and your car is forcing you to be a good driver!

What is even more galling are all the roadside signs, which read:

'WE TRUST YOU NOT TO SPEED.'

and:

'WE KNOW YOU WON'T LITTER.'

You come to a drive-in theatre. There on screen, playing for the entire crowd, is your life.

You are a movie star.

No-one is watching the story of your life. No-one even has the speakers turned on.

The cafeteria has shut. Outside it there is a machine which dispenses fortune cookies. You buy one, and open it.

Inside is a mirror.

The film runs off at the end of roll two (about the time you were applying unsuccessfully for your first job). The projectionist has passed out with boredom. You were the only person watching your past life and it looked even worse in replay than it seemed at the time.

A man comes up to your car selling candy, popcorn and next-lives. He is offering Nobel prize-winners, Olympic athletes, movie stars and world leaders. You fumble in your pockets for loose change. You have spent most of your money on the Corniche.

The person-pedlar frowns, realising his chance of a commission is dim. He offers you lawyers, car salesmen, and telephone repair persons.

'CHEAP!'

Still your hand jangles emptily in your pants.

The salesman of soon-to-be-people realises he is dealing with a real lower-shelf type. Wearily he recommends the bargain basement beings: politicians, journalists, Chief Executive Officers, and publicity officers for tobacco companies.

Your hand finally grasps the errant coinage. The purveyor of predestination pries your fingers apart, takes the dull coppers, examines them sadly and replaces them with a small catalogue.

'Pick one!'

he sighs deeply.

You glance down. It is a book of exquisite photographs. Truly exquisite photographs.

Of salamanders.

So it has come to this. You have made all the wrong choices.

You are about to be reincarnated not even as a human, but as a small, short-sighted lizard covered with mucus.

The pages of the salamander catalogue become strangely reflective. Your face is merged with the image of the amphibian — just so you can begin to get used to the idea.

You scream.

The tout from tomorrowland leaves you, and approaches the adjoining car where he is promptly involved in a *ménage à trois* with a couple who plan to torture animals in their next lives.

You reverse the Corniche desperately out of the drive-in, back to the freeway, past the patronising road signs, to the Mikimoto Pearly Gates. You throw the keys and the payment book for the Corniche at the Bagwan, and as you head back to Earth you hear his dulcet tones murmur:

'Get a life!'

You are determined to be kind and good, optimistic and happy, full of *joie de vivre*, an inspiration to all mankind.

Heaven can wait!

You come to on the operating table. The doctors have managed, it seems, to bring you out of anaesthetic trauma with no side effects. You have had a near-death experience and lived.

The doctors give you a good three years before your 'condition' will require their services again. You are so happy you forget what your 'condition' was and treat yourself to a take-away curry.

From the Ridiculous to the Divine

(Becoming a Demi-god of Failure)

Chapter 18

While it may have simply been indigestion from the celebratory tandoori prawns, nevertheless something sparks inside you after your near-death experience, and you decide to tell the world what you have seen so they, too, can become better people. So they can become less concerned about Earthly failure.

But to do this you must take the Bagwan's advice, or no-one, especially failures, will listen to you.

You must become a Demi-god of Failure. Below is a step-by-step guide to achieving your goal, and how to create a truly absurd belief system in the process.

Step-by-step Guide to Becoming a Demi-god of Failure

Step 1. Examine the field. It is going to be tough; already there's a middle-aged apiarist, a tuna fisherman from Sweden, a ginseng farmer from Wollongong, and a science-fiction writer whose books sound like love poems to guinea fowl, who are all claiming to be demi-gods. And that's only in the time since you thought of the idea!

Step 2. Develop an idiotic icon for your cult. Crystals have, unfortunately, been done. In fact, most minerals have been snapped up by loons from other foolish faiths.

However, Edwardian dining room tables are a possibility as a spiritual lodestone for your religion. You may initially wonder if *anyone* could believe that locked inside polished mahogany lies ultimate knowledge. It seems not *quite* as silly, and may therefore not be *quite* as successful as your opposition's claims that lumps of amethyst can cure genital warts, or that your labrador once lunched with you in the last century. Remember, however, that Edwardian dining room tables *are* expensive, and that means they will probably attract their fair share of devotees. And they can *only* be Edwardian dining room tables which have been 'harmonised' by the demi-god! (Which will add significantly to the price.)

Step 3. Choose your proper prophet title.

(a) It should begin either with 'The Blessed', 'The Universal', or 'The Omnipotent'. 'Blessed' may be too old fashioned, and 'Omnipotent' casts aspersions on your sex drive (for, after all, there must be lots of demi-godlike sex in this cult!).

(b) Following 'The Universal' must come a statement which ties you to somebody very important, like Buddha, Shiva, Adam or Eve. You choose the Pharaoh Ramses because you like the sound of 'ram' and think it will tip those undecided on demi-godlike sex over the line.

(c) Next choose a word which no-one has ever heard of, but which sounds exotic. Like 'phlemhacker'.

(d) And finally, to accent your demi-*human* state, you must affix your surname to the whole thing.

Thus all pronouncements on spiritual matters now come from the blessed and omnipotent mouth of The Universal Ramses Phlemhacker Jones.

Step 4. The final step is to write the creed for your new religion. This is normally not difficult, as long as you remember the two golden rules of convincing others of your demi-divine status. Your mandate for spiritual advancement must firstly contain *no* logical thought and, secondly, *must* use lots of silly words.

By following this plan you will soon have a flock of full-blown religious loons and whackos who will do your every bidding — who have shelled over oodles of cash for Edwardian dining room tables with which they 'harmonise' to achieve the exalted spiritual status of POTDIRT (Possessor Of The Dining Room Table). It may trouble you briefly that your family are at the front of the pack, but remember that failure begets failure.

It is important now, in order to strengthen your store-front religion, to put your disciples to work. If the law allows, whip them, but in any case maltreat them as much as you can. Don't worry — they will lap it up, just ask a Moonie! Instil your flock with paranoia and, most importantly, create an enemy which just happens to include anyone who is not in your cult. Tell your disciples that instead of petrol, most service stations pump acid into their cars and affix listening devices under the hood. Who is responsible for this evil?

THE OTHERS!

The Others are responsible for everything bad; from rotten peaches to leprosy, from faulty spark plugs to 'Don't Walk' signals which happen just as you want to walk . . .

You have succeeded. Your cult grows. Thousands join your flock — from everywhere, of all the gin-joint cults in all the cities of the world, they choose yours.

At every major international airport your disciples have bundled out the Hare Krishnas and are handing out short pamphlets entitled '*The Complete Wisdom of The Universal Ramses Phlemhacker Jones*'.

You make the cover of *Time* magazine!

You are elevated from Demi-god to Living God.

Then you realise how conclusively you have been duped. How your utter, complete, and everlasting failure has been achieved.

Having become a Living God there is nowhere else to go. You are destined to be endlessly reincarnated as the same Living God.

That is — yourself. Over, and over, and over, and over, and over, and over . . . As yourself.

You are a failure not only in this life, but also the next; and the one after that, too. The Eternal Failure. Well done!

Appendix

Coping with Joy — Miserable Mantras to Mutter

At some point in their lives even the most complete failure can become infected with the cancer of optimism.

There you will be, walking along the street, bumping into people and singing 'Yeah baby yeah!' to your walkman . . . in short, feeling perfectly miserable. When suddenly, out of the blue, someone will come up, unannounced, and be friendly to you! Or the sun will come out from behind the clouds and your spirit will soar because someone smiles at you!

Or the toll collector will grin at you through the car window and say:

'Don't worry about it today, son, I'm feeling generous.'

You will probably be curious about the strange emotion you feel.

It is joy.

And it is dangerous!

You haven't spent all that money on this book, and all those hours alone in your room learning how to become a Fast-track Failure, only to let it all go out the window because some jerk-off toll collector is feeling magnanimous, have you?

No! These moments of passing joy must be stomped on and curtailed as quickly as possible! If you are a *truly* successful failure, your best method of eclipsing optimism when it occurs is to attempt to be warm and friendly (in the certain knowledge that you will fail at this task). The toll collector will soon come to his senses and take your licence plate to report you for attempted bribery of a public official.

However, if the *slightest* doubt exists in your mind that you may not quite be at the nadir of failuredom, memorise the following off-putting phrases and use them as liberally as necessary to deter other, happy, people from talking, smiling or sharing the footpath with you . . . or simply to quash the occasional spark of hope which may, from time to time, flicker in your breast.

Coping with joy is never easy, but these miserable mantras should help.

While the following should be uttered in a normal conversational tone, or muttered to yourself, it is quite acceptable to shout them, print them on your T-shirt or underwear, or write them on posters to paste around your home and office. We have categorised them for ease of reference.

OFF-PUTTING RESPONSES

To be spoken aloud to people attempting to speak or show a little human kindness to you.

- 'Don't talk to me, you'll only regret it.'
- 'I don't mean to be rude, but I'm having a bad life.'
- 'I have no redeeming features.'
- 'I'm not sure I was present at my birth.'
- 'I am hated by my pets.'
- 'Yes — feel good! You could be me.'
- 'You don't want to know me.'
- 'I may look like a fool but I dance like a blender.'
- 'I'm a total tragedy.'
- 'Wanna hear about my medical problem?'
- 'I've lost my ticket to ride.'
- 'The only point to life is the one my head ends in.'
- 'I write bad poetry about chickens.'
- 'I hang around hospitals.'
- 'Depressed until you met me, weren't you?'
- 'I'm a free-range idiot.'
- 'I suspect I was Shirley MacLaine in my last life.'
- 'I know the meaning of life . . . unfortunately.'

- 'I decided not to reproduce, for humanitarian reasons.'
- 'I'm an actor I hired to play me.'
- 'I don't understand checkers.'
- 'I worship the wrong god.'
- 'My friends helped me have a near-death experience.'
- 'I fell on my head as a child.'
- 'I model my life on Barry Manilow songs.'

SAD THOUGHTS FOR THE DAY

To be repeated to yourself before arising from bed in the morning.

- 'Today will be bad.'
- 'For me every day is Friday the 13th.'
- 'God short-changed me.'
- 'Get out there and seize destiny by the ankles!'
- 'In the march of mankind, I'm gum on the pavement.'
- 'I may be attacked today.'
- 'I am, therefore I'm not sure.'
- 'There is something wrong with me.'
- 'I'm not playing with a full deck.'
- 'No man is an island . . . I'm a deep sea trough.'
- 'I am a Fast-track Failure.'
- 'I am the recipe for disaster.'
- 'On the fifth day He made me, then He made lizards.'
- 'There are no answers . . . at least none I can understand.'
- 'There has to be a problem for every solution.'
- 'I bet I was myself in the last life too.'
- 'It can only get worse.'
- 'Evolution passed me by.'
- 'I'm a pale imitation.'
- 'My mind is a blank.'
- 'I'll try and fail.'
- 'I'm the flip side.'
- 'I'm an ersatz individual.'
- 'Today will be my worst day . . . so far.'

DESOLATE EPITHETS, CHEERLESS CATCHPHRASES AND MOROSE MESSAGES

To be scrawled on T-shirts, underwear, and 'Post-it' Notes attached to your forehead.

- 'I am "Conception — Worst Case Scenario".'
- 'If you're knocked down, stay there.'
- 'For a free course in mind-numbing conversation, say "Hello".'
- 'Hire me, I will make you look good.'
- 'It's a small world . . . you'll have no idea how small unless you talk to me.'
- 'Depression isn't so bad . . . it's worse!'
- 'My reason for living is an artichoke.'
- 'Member — Young Embalmers Guild.'
- 'Young, white and terminally dull.'
- 'Back off! I might talk to you.'
- 'I'm as useful as last year's calendar.'
- 'Join A.F.A. (Athlete's Foot Anonymous).'
- 'Be a loser, not a fighter!'
- 'Trainee newt!'
- 'I'm supported by a family in India.'
- 'Beware — I ask stupid questions.'
- 'Clean fill wanted.'
- 'Don't let me use your cutlery.'
- 'Stop the merry-go-round!'
- 'You knew me at high school.'